Dr. Roy G. Biv; Healing from Trauma One Colorful Painting at a Time, An Artist's Journey to Hope and Joy

First Published in 2024 by Platapus Publishing

Copyright © Katie Southworth, 2024

All Rights Reserved. No part of this publication may be reproduced, stored or transmitted in any form or by any means, electronic, mechanical, photocopying, recorder, scanning, or otherwise without written permission from the publisher. It is illegal to copy this book, post it to a website, or distribute it by any other means without permission.

Cover and Interior Design by Olivia Piazza
Front and Back Cover Photography by Matthew and Michael Moloney
Author Photograph by Matthew and Michael Moloney

All included artwork and creative writing © Katie Southworth 2021 2022 2023 and 2024

Dr. Roy G. Biv

Healing from Trauma One Colorful Painting at a Time, An Artist's Journey to Hope and Joy.

Memoir, Artworks, and Creative Writing

By Katie Southworth

For my mother, Ellie.
I miss you, but I love you more.

Table of Contents

PREFACE	8
MY STORY	10
ABOUT THE WORK	32
ART & WRITING	34
On Joy	36
Lessons From Nature	66
On Adversity & Loss	112
On Humanness & Wellness	146
On Personal Growth & Career	182
On Love	216
ACKNOWLEDGEMENTS	240
ABOUT THE ARTIST	244

Preface

No, "Dr. Roy G. Biv" is not a real person!
Remember that acronym you learned in grade school?

Red
Orange
Yellow

Green

Blue
Indigo
Violet

The Doctor may be fake, but the healing power of color is real. I am living proof. But I promise, this book is not all about sunshine and rainbows! Rather, it's about how I learned to dance in the rain, and the lemonade I made with the lemons. I wrote it for you, whether you love color or not.

If you are anything like me, we have at least one of these in common:

You are ambitious, empathetic, sensitive, and strong.
You have loved and lost.
You have been told you are "wise beyond your years."
You find comfort in music, writing, or art.
You get goosebumps from watching a colorful sunrise.
You miss someone who took their life.
You wonder if you are grieving "correctly."
You feel alone sometimes, even when surrounded by people.
You know you deserve joy and happiness, but it's been elusive.
You struggle to find time for self-care, play, and fun.
You have a creative side that fluctuates between active and dormant.
You have a good job but crave something more meaningful.
Your ultimate goal is to thrive in a happy, healthy life.

I wrote this book to show you that you are not alone. I lost my mother to suicide when I was 21. Today, at 30, I am a full-time artist using color to heal and grieve, as well as promote mental wellness and hope for others. I arrived at this healthy place of passion and purpose only after navigating tumultuous career shifts, an internal battle with self-care, and a worldwide pandemic!

Even if you have never picked up a paintbrush, you will find bits and pieces of yourself in my story, and perhaps find inspiration to forge your own way forward. I have leaned into vulnerability and offered you a front-row seat to my story of loss and journey with grieving. My healing method is unconventional, and that's ok. In fact, that's the point! My story offers hope that unique paths exist and are worth pursuing.

Inside these pages, I share nearly 100 of my favorite colorful paintings and complementary statements with you. For the first time, I have presented my work organized in themes that have recurred over the last three years, instead of by series. Get ready for expressions on everything from the joys of nature to adversity and loss.

My goal is not to insist that color is the key to happiness. Rather, color is *my* joy, and I included a ton of it in here so you could try it on for size. I am thrilled to share my passion with you. And while I hope you come away with a newfound appreciation for color and its power to uplift you, it's ok if you don't. What matters is that you keep trying joyful things until you connect with something that works for you.

Speaking of connection, whether you are completely new to my story, or you have been there since the beginning, this book is here to help us foster a deeper bond and build a stronger community. There is strength in numbers and coming together over shared experiences. If something in these pages resonates with you, please share away! I welcome you to reach out and tell me about it, tell friends and family, give the book as a gift, or post about it. Please tag me on Instagram @katiesouthworth_art and follow along to find more amazing people like yourself.

Sharing art that sets you free is a powerful way to find folks who will fuel your soul.

Trust me, I know!

My Story

There are seven billion stories in the world currently unfolding, and this one is the beginning of mine. A happy upbringing turned into an early adulthood of unexpected adversity and an unprecedented world crisis. Career goals were set, and then changed, morphed again, and then turned into something I never imagined. I am who I am now because I found a way to put my mental health first and to choose joy amid omnipresent darkness.

THE EARLY DAYS

When I was young, I used to joke that painting was my retirement plan. Maybe that's because I grew up with a potter as a paternal grandmother and a painter as a maternal great-grandmother. Whatever the reason, I grew up spending more time dreaming about becoming an Olympic gymnast than anything.

I was the kid who could not, for the life of her, sit still. My parents, Ken and Ellie, raised my younger brother, Alden, and me in Darien, Connecticut. They met and fell in love on Martha's Vineyard as teenagers, so we spent at least a small chunk of every summer there. But no matter where we were, my restlessness prevailed. So I was plopped in gymnastics class as soon as possible, at the ripe age of three. By age seven, I had abs that showed through my shirt, biceps bigger than all the boys, and the hands of a longshoreman. They were helpful in the gym, and to give my dad a solid chuckle, but they didn't last forever. Instead, gymnastics is how I learned (and never forgot) a strong work ethic, focus, discipline, patience, delayed gratification, mental and physical strength, how to develop life-long relationships, and, most importantly, what true joy, love, and passion feel like.

My mother, having been a former gymnast herself, was rapt in reliving her glory days as we spent years traveling the country, competing with my teammates. It was the crux of our bond for most of our lives together. My friends from the gym will often remind me how many decibels louder than the rest of the crowd my mother would cheer, not just for me, but for everyone on my team. Or, heck, for the daughter of whoever was sitting next to her. Mom was different, but it wasn't just her enthusiasm that made her stand out from the crowd.

Ellie's most iconic feature was that she could talk to anyone, and she did so any chance she could. People at the gym, at school, at the grocery store, at restaurants (mostly the busy waiters who didn't have time), cabbies, receptionists, and random people on the street. Literally anyone, anywhere. To say she had the gift of the gab was an understatement. She would get lost in conversation, losing complete track of time. We used to tell her white lies about arrival and departure times 30 minutes earlier than scheduled just to have a chance of arriving anywhere on time. And as inconvenient as that could be at times, the beauty is what I remember most: whoever she was talking to was nearly always smiling.

People appreciated Ellie because she had this unique ability to wake them up, make them laugh, and be excited about their own lives. When she asked you how you were and what was going on, she actually meant it, and would actively listen to your response. And then she would celebrate you with this fervor that often stopped people in their tracks. They would look at her with this pleasantly confused expression as if to say "I don't know why you're being this nice to me but thank you, I needed this." Of course, they weren't all winners. Sometimes her enthusiasm hit people the wrong way, her curiosity could be inappropriately placed, and her joie-de-vivre sometimes, well, put her in a pickle a time or two.

In short, at times Ellie's eccentrism was exactly what I, another human, or a whole room, needed. Other times, it was a bit too much. She was the source of my joy and my embarrassment all at the same time, as good mothers are. Ellie just had this enduring light inside of her, and she uplifted everything and everyone around her. Fittingly, she wore bright-colored clothing most of the time, and would often tell me, "I really wish you wouldn't wear black." I assumed it was just her preference, but I was completely unaware of the depth of meaning, let alone the foreshadowing. Just being her daughter, and watching her all the time, she taught me so much about people, and nothing about art.

I was extraordinarily lucky to have fantastic art teachers, every year of my K-12 public school education, and art sat comfortably as my favorite elective in school. My father likes to think that this is because it was the one place in which I didn't have to compete at all, and I have a hard time disagreeing with that theory. I loved learning about new materials and using my brain and body in a new way. Honestly, I was rarely restless while creating something.

By the time I reached freshman year at Darien High School, I was forced to resign from year-round gymnastics because it was breaking my body. I was both crushed by the loss of my first true love and desperate to put my competitive, insatiable energy somewhere new. So I transformed into a fiercely competitive student-athlete, taking up varsity swimming, the high school gymnastics team (couldn't stay away), and varsity track and field as a pole vaulter... (ah, youth). I also took AP English Language, Honors Physics, AP AB Calculus, and AP Studio Art. While I was often commended for zealously tackling a full schedule of such demanding courses and sports, it came at a price. I struggled greatly with balance, seldom slept, and pushed myself in every mentally and physically detrimental way to get into a top-notch university. My father scolded me more frequently for being up in the middle of the night studying, as opposed to acting out or partying (of which I did very little). Once, my brother got up for his 5am hockey practice and found me still awake studying for a test that day, at which time he informed me, "It's a snow day, idiot, go to bed."

Ironically enough, even though they were a lot less stressful, my art classes received the same work ethic, and I got pretty good at it. In March 2012, I got the news that I had been accepted into Colby College. Ecstatic, I also finally relaxed a bit and managed to enjoy the last chunk of high school. At this time, I was also doing particularly well in my AP studio art course. This was enough to initially spark my interest in continuing to study art in college. What solidified the idea was the awareness (in my newfound, semi-relaxed era), that I genuinely enjoy it, and maybe it's time I do more of what I find enjoyable even if it isn't necessarily productive or high achieving. I had worked so hard up to this point, and I remember thinking that I should give myself more time for play, fun, and rest.

STUDYING COLOR

Long before arriving at Colby, I knew I wanted to Major in Psychology. I was interested in it at least in part because of the human interactions I both observed and experienced having Ellie as a mother. Unfortunately, I also experienced several scary scenarios with friends who struggled with mental health, substance abuse, and extreme anxiety in high school. I suppose, starting at a young age, I was eager to understand what made people the way they were. I wanted to know where joy and happiness came from, how personality and emotions worked, and what caused pain and suffering too. I expected to learn that, and I did. What I did not expect was to accidentally become a studio art major as well.

This all started by weaseling my way into Painting 1 as a freshman. Foundations of Studio Art was technically required as a prerequisite, but in reading the course description it listed skills I knew I already had. My score of 4 on the AP calculus exam had relieved me of my college math requirement. Perhaps my high score on the AP Art exam could count towards something as well. So I asked politely, and the painting professor, Bevin, invited me in for a portfolio review. I happily accepted. With this little extra effort and self-advocacy, my wish was granted. Boom, there I sat, the only freshman in Painting 1.

I'll be honest, in addition to genuine interest, I thought taking painting classes would also be a fun way to keep my GPA up at a very rigorous college. I quickly learned that there's no such thing as an easy course at Colby, and it was more frustrating than fun for the first two years. Bevin, who I am eternally grateful for, just so happens to be particularly ruthless with her instruction on - you guessed it - color. And I needed every bit of it. I was terrible with color at first.. in the bottom of the class, at some points. But remember that crazy gymnast spirit? It never wanes. I had to master it.

I went through tubes and tubes of paint, ruined plenty of panels, broke a few palette knives, and dropped more than a few "colorful" words along the way. I made paintings I still genuinely despise to this day. Of course, this is what learning is, doing it poorly until you do it well. But in other subjects, you don't end up with visual depictions of your ineptitude at the end of your lesson! Despite the struggle, eventually, I made some headway. I still have the painting where Bevin looked at it, looked at me, and said "Katie, you're going to want to keep this one forever, this is a breakthrough." But let me just add here, to this day I'm still working on it. Color is just like that. It's a never-ending teacher in its vastness and complexity. As Bevin says, "Through the eye of the needle there is truly a universe." She couldn't have been more on the nose. If color is my Force, she was my Yoda.

By the time my studies allowed me to take my working knowledge of color and apply it to my own creative ideas and interests, (Junior year), I hit another wall. What am I interested in?? Everything! Art history classes had opened my brain wide open in terms of everything that could be expressed with paint. I managed to figure out that I was more interested in abstraction than anything, but my paintings at this point remained confused, focusless, and scattered in conception, technique, and execution. You can check Bevin's comments on my portfolio reviews for proof. Although frustrating, this is an important and meaningful stage in any artist's life, and I am grateful that I had this one. It's important to explore and let yourself be a beginner, often. True authenticity is born from painstaking, internal wayfinding.

Speaking of discovery, it was around this time that my brother and I were let in on a big family secret. He had been accepted into Colby as well by the way, (what a kid), and we were both home for Christmas break when our mother sat us down in the dining room, (which was already odd, so I remember feeling a lump in my stomach before she said a word). One of our cousins had been acting very strange about a month prior, and Mom knew Alden and I were concerned. She explained that our cousin was experiencing an episode of something called mania, which diagnosed them as someone living with Bipolar I. But that wasn't all. She said that it hadn't surprised her because Bipolar Disorder can be genetic… and then her voice broke, right before she got to the truth: she had been living with Bipolar II herself for most of her life.

First I remember feeling empathy for her, but it was mixed with this academic thought of "Oh… that makes sense." I hadn't had the chance to study it in school yet, but I knew enough to understand that it explained a lot of what made her different. The way she seemed to exist in a more elevated state of exuberance than most people in a room. Then I felt scared and sad because at this point she began to cry. Up until now, my brother and I were completely unaware of her depressive episodes and how scary they could be. This was due to a combination of two facts, one good, and one bad. The good: she and her doctors managed her illness very well, and she had very few low bouts. The bad: through the ones she did have, she was a stubborn, silent, soldier. All my intellectual deflection mechanisms suddenly went out the window. I was just a daughter learning that her mother was sick. And it hurt like all hell.

She apologized for keeping it a secret and admitted that she had meant to tell us sooner, but was afraid we would see her differently. This is the crushing power of stigma. Naturally, we hugged her, thanked her for telling us, and told her of course we didn't and wouldn't see or treat her differently. We loved her how she was. As for me, I looked forward to taking Abnormal Psychology next fall, in hopes of understanding this part of her a bit better.

Junior year ended, and I was still struggling with paint. I remember hesitantly adding Painting IV to my schedule for senior fall, not knowing that this was when I would finally find my area of interest, style, and voice. I just wish the way that I found it was different. It happened because of another event that I wish never occurred. I would trade it all, give up my entire artistic identity and career, to reverse the thing that launched it.

THAT DAY

It was the last Friday in August 2015, the summer between my junior and senior years at Colby. Mom and Alden had left Martha's Vineyard to get ready for school on Tuesday of that week. I stayed to finish up my summer job as a waitress. I remember her saying "Get home safe," and thinking it was weird that she didn't say "See you at home." My Friday evening shift had just started and the house was packed when the hostess came running up to me with the restaurant's landline and said, "Someone needs to talk to you, I think it's important."

"Hello?"

"Kate.." unmistakably my brother's voice, I would know it anywhere, but it was shaky and terrified.

"Alden? What's wrong?"

After a painstaking, tearful, pause, he finally musters,

"..Mom is dead."

I can't remember if I screamed internally or aloud at this point because my brain was so intensely disturbed with confusion. "That just doesn't make any sense," I remember thinking. Regardless, somehow he knew to elaborate.

"She killed herself..."

Then, I remember my eyes glazing over, the brain fog going away, the whirlwind shifting to my stomach, and thinking "fuck... *that* makes sense." Terrible, heart-stopping, sense. With clarity on what had happened, at that moment, I was doubled over, somehow managed to say "I'm coming home," before dropping the phone, collapsing to the ground in the middle of the restaurant, and scream-sobbing in that soundless, airless, empty kind of way. I don't know how much time went by or how they got me to sit in a chair, but my coworkers finally got me to speak, and before I knew it they had helped me find the rest of my family and we instantly went home to Connecticut.

I spent the whole flight toggling between disbelief, heartbreak, and feeling like a failure for not saying something. I couldn't stop thinking about that first thought I'd had. The, "that makes sense" thought. It crushed me. I had watched her suffer through a dismal low all summer long, knowing she wasn't ok but innocently believing she would get better, having faith that she and her doctor had it under control. I was 21, with eight months of knowledge that she even battled a disease at all, and it was my first time witnessing her in a depression. I didn't have anything to compare it to, but I remember feeling a cold, knowing, terror in my bones that I didn't know what to do with. Should I say something? No, too scary, and I don't think I know what I'm talking about. Deny the possibility and focus on hope for healing? The latter seemed like the better choice for me at the time, but now I wish I had been braver and called for help.

The truth is, the shoulda-coulda-woulda thoughts are never helpful, and I know it's not my fault. But to anyone that's ever had that horrific gut feeling that feels too scary to even acknowledge, and had the unfortunate experience of being right... I hate knowing what it feels like but I do. And all I can do is wish I could jump through these pages and hug you. It's dark, heavy, and haunting. You are not alone... and I also hate that. I hate just how considerably we are not alone. It is all too common.

You have two options when something like this happens to you. You can get back on the horse of life and commit to grieving and healing as you go, or you can try to press pause for a while. And as much as you can pause certain things (and completely respect and support those who do), only one option felt right for me and my brother. After all, the carousel of life never stops turning. Bereft as we were, we decided we would go back to Colby on time. At least we would be together on campus, which all of a sudden felt like it was eerily predestined.

Unfortunately, that decision meant we had a measly two weeks. Those two weeks forced my family to go through every impossibly difficult decision under the sun in an absurdly fast fashion. Everything from accepting what had happened, to planning a service, writing eulogies, saying goodbye, and figuring out how to keep going with life. No one had any idea if it was right or wrong, it was just happening. A theme that would continue, I learned.

Spoiler alert: I'm still figuring it out. I think we all are.

While I prefer to keep my memory of Mom's service private, I will share one story of the day after. My father went to our church's parish to donate some of her things. The volunteer says to my dad,

"Good thing you didn't come yesterday, my gosh, I've never seen this place so packed. It must have been some sort of celebrity that died. Do you know who that was for?"

"Yes. It was for my wife," he says, as all the blood drains from her face.

"Oh my God.. I am so sorry. I feel awful. Your wife must have been very important... what did she do?" she asks, still curious.

"...she was nice to people," he says, as honestly as honest is.

EARLY ADULTHOOD IN "THE AFTER"

That first year she was gone I went through three huge milestones. Two of these I expected: graduating college, and entering the working world. Navigating this without her was... complex. Of course, it was heartbreaking, sad, and impossible in ways, but there was also beauty, clarity, strength, magic, and empowerment.

I'm obnoxious like that now. I'm the queen of finding the good in terrible situations. I think it's because I've seen the consequences of turning attention to the darkest part of things, and I'd rather find out what happens when you do the opposite. Again, two choices, always. See the good or see the bad. Be kind or be mean. Do good or do evil. Call for help or stay silent. Whenever there's a choice, nowadays I tend to air on the positive or safe side. Call it being my mother's daughter, or call it a trauma response. It's probably both. Potato, potahto. At the same time, "toxic positivity" is its own evil, and I don't do that either. Anyway, I digress. Here's what happened in the early years of my life in "The After."

PART 1: SENIOR YEAR

On paper, there was a lot in place that made it seem like I would be surrounded by support. And I was. After all, Colby is an amazingly tight-knit community of under 2,000 students. I was a leader on the varsity swim team which met multiple times a day. I had great friends. I attended classes every day with professors who actually knew and cared about me. Plus, I had mandated therapy. And if that wasn't enough people just in sheer quantity, I also had top quality with my brother on campus. So, while I was indeed surrounded, the first word that pops into my mind when I think of this year is: lonely.

Maybe one can suggest that this was because I lived alone, my college boyfriend had graduated the year before, and most of my academic work demanded focused alone time. But I don't think any of that mattered. I was simply brand new at being a motherless daughter, and a suicide survivor. Which, I learned, is inherently, internally isolating. It's as noticeable as walking around without an arm and a leg. But instead of a limb, it's your irreplaceable, umbilical, sublime source of unconditional love and knowledge of oneself, womanhood, and life itself. It's a bit like navigating a new road blindfolded. Or, if you have chosen to keep going with life as it spins like I had, it's a bit more like building a plane while you're flying it. Solo. And oh yeah, God just threw out the instruction manual.

Ironically, the alone time was exactly what I needed. It was painful, but it also gave me space to grieve as I saw fit, without anyone looking or judging, which turned out to be way more effective than sitting in front of a stranger who I didn't even get to select myself and trying to talk about it. This is the part where I admit that I quit my mandated therapy almost immediately. Important sidebar, I fully believe in and advocate for therapy. I have been back since college, and I think everyone could benefit. But at this time, when I had 1,000 responsibilities, a packed schedule, and no time to myself, the most effective way of healing was simply letting myself grieve on my own and listening to my feelings. I wasn't ready for therapy yet.

Most often, (other than binging Grey's Anatomy in my room, which was comforting but admittedly unproductive), my solo grieving happened in the studio. Today, I think a lot about how grateful I am to have had painting on my schedule that fall, ready to rescue me. Remember when I said I found my voice senior year? In all fairness, it was more like a full year of discovery, but it was all kicked off with a lightbulb moment I'll never forget.

I was sitting in what I believe was my very first painting class of that fall semester. It was time to decide on a direction for a new painting, but I was having trouble. Bevin, who knew what I'd just been through, suggested I warm up with some "simple color studies." Sure, what the hell. I was just grateful someone had a productive idea. I decided to observe an object and create a line of paint for each color I saw within it. My best guess for why I picked lines was because at this time I was particularly inspired by Mark Rothko and Richard Deibenkorn.

Anyway, after about five "studies" it hit me... this was it. Simple color and light. That's it. That's what makes things complex, interesting, and beautiful to me. Not the shape, texture, form, etc., all that just confuses me. I was fascinated by the world that opened up within comparing and contrasting solely the raw color of things, which was of course always influenced by the light on it. I reveled in the vastness within the limitations. It's amazing, the complexity of a thing when you spend some truly mindful time with it.

The next thing I discovered was how the width of a line was a perfect but perplexing tool to indicate the importance of a particular color, or how much of it you needed to keep a piece balanced, harmonious, but still representative of your idea. Then, to figure out where to place that line... next to which existing color... that was a whole other world of thought. Everything is relative, after all. A cool blue looks a whole heck of a lot differently when placed next to a warm orange than when placed next to a cool purple (to put it simply). On top of all that, my professor made sure to remind me often that I would only get the strongest and truest color comparison if the lines were super, crispy clean. I finally understood what Bevin meant by "through the eye of the needle there is truly a universe." Well, I had found my universe, and I was hooked.

Essentially, I had invented my own game of creating and solving a colorful puzzle. And when I did them well, the paintings represented the essence of something complex in a calming, uplifting way. It was the form of abstraction I was chasing all along. It's wild to describe in words. I wonder if it makes any sense to describe it this way at all. I also wonder if Bevin laughed inside when she suggested I pursue "simple color studies." She knew there was nothing simple about it at all. I love her for that.

Anyway, what they looked like is less important than the point: I had reached clarity on what I was interested in. In the same way that one can gain clarity on what's important in life after a major tragedy or loss, I found clarity on what was important to me in painting. On what I wanted to constantly study, chase, and hopefully capture. And I don't think it's any coincidence that this happened to me weeks after losing my mother.

I followed this curiosity all year. But I was hit with another surprise in the middle of it, positive this time. Just before the start of senior Spring, my advisor called me into her office. She says,

"You know, because you started with Painting 1, if you just take one extra class this Spring, you could end up with a double major.. psychology and studio art."

Interesting… *over-achiever mentality kicks in*.

"Ok, let's do it." I concede.

"Great! Oh, and you'll have to participate in the Senior Capstone Exhibition," she adds as if it's just a simple, fine-print clause.

"As in I'll have to show my work at the end of the year? To people? Formally?" I ask for clarity.

"Yes, but it's a high honor, a very professional event, and a great way to get formal exhibition experience under your belt," she explains, as my over-achiever mentality fully surrenders.

"I guess I'm an art major now… huh."

(This was the third milestone, by the way. The one that I did not expect. My first formal art show.)

By May, I had created about 12 paintings that I was very pleased with. With my professor's help, I selected a curation of seven to feature in the show. Each one was titled after a joyful person, place, or thing that it reminded me of, and I titled the series "Lights of my Life." I wrote a statement about how they were dedicated to and inspired by my mom, and how much the paintings helped me grieve her.

There was a particularly poignant moment regarding Mom while creating the series. I was in the middle of a pink and orange piece. I was stuck on it and had been staring at it for a long time. And then, out of nowhere, I just started sobbing. With cathartic tears streaming down my face, I realized that pink and orange were precisely Ellie's aura: warm, energetic, fun, loving, beautiful, and strong. I could feel her love coming to me through the piece. That was the first time that happened. To this day, pink and orange are what I use to channel her during the best and worst of times when I miss her most.

On Opening Night, I remember an overwhelming outpouring of support. Family, friends, teammates, coaches, professors, and peers were all there to celebrate with me. I was honestly stunned, but mostly grateful because I also felt stark naked with vulnerability (which is saying something coming from someone who performed in either a leotard or a bathing suit all her life). But the moment that truly knocked me off my feet was when I was awarded the Charles Hovey Pepper Prize, the only merit-based scholarship award presented by the Studio Art Department, for my work. As the whole room cheered for me, the cognitive dissonance of "winning" in something other than sports and school set in. It had nothing to do with winning an award, and everything to do with being valued for something new. Most significantly, it forced me to pause and notice the moment, to feel what it felt like to have others find worth in something that I thought was only important to me.

That was the first time I thought to myself "I think... I might be an artist." I remember telling my professor that, and her insisting I start introducing myself that way. She was certain, but it would be a while before I had the nerve to do this. Still, it was in my brain. Identity is a funny thing we are all constantly evolving, and it's hard to pinpoint exact moments. This was one such moment.

By the way, at this point, the only people who had seen my work were physically at the show. I wasn't posting about them, sharing my work online, or talking about it much at all. No one else knew I was an artist but me and the people in that room. And I was about to graduate in a few weeks to start a career in education. In other words, I had about two seconds to realize I was an artist before the next phase of my life began. (The carousel never stops turning!) So my shiny new artist identity was swiftly pushed to the back burner. But luckily, thanks to the show, it wasn't taken off the stove completely.

PART 2: EARLY POST-GRAD YEARS

I moved to Boston almost immediately after graduation, into my first crappy apartment, with three roommates I had never met before. I didn't care that the roof leaked; it was a new home in which to create a new life. All four of us were signed up for a 10-month, Americorps service year with City Year. I accepted the job in the early fall of my Senior year. I remember thinking that my plans to pursue a profession in psychology were moot because anything in the clinical field now felt way too close to home. I figured education was a safe field in which to get my feet wet. I loved kids, hated sitting down, and I was good at public speaking. Beyond that, I had little knowledge of what to expect.

Well, we quickly learned that City Year was absurdly hard work, crazy long hours, and our stipends and food stamps barely kept us afloat in a big city. We did nothing but work. I kept an old ironing board in the corner of my room to occasionally make tiny color studies, but in actuality barely made anything at all. Luckily, loved ones who knew me best did a good job reminding me of my idling artistic side. My dad wanted me to take piano lessons. My brother asked for a painting for his dorm room. My favorite story: my then-boyfriend sent me a link on that Christmas morning. It took me to my first art website, my name in the URL, that he had purchased and set up himself. I have a different website today, but that first one was easily one of the best gifts I have ever received. Even still, although very much in sight, art remained on the back burner.

Instead, every day, donned in my red jacket, I assistant-taught in my assigned 4th-grade classroom at the Trotter Innovation School on Humboldt Avenue in Roxbury, MA. I worked directly with small groups of focus-list students on attendance, behavior, and coursework. One of my boys learned to love reading after starting the year afraid to try. Another girl learned to love coming to school with a smile after spending the fall sleeping through half of each day. My favorite moment was when one of my girls defended her answer in math with full, enthusiastic confidence to the entire class (of 70% boys), even though her answer was different than anyone else's. She was right.

Despite these great moments, the biggest career takeaway of City Year happened because I elected to start an afterschool art club at my school (which did not have an art teacher). In giving these kids a chance to create, emote, play, express, and experiment, that they otherwise wouldn't have, I noticed such tremendous potential for social-emotional growth and healing. Some would come to the club in a post-school-day, tiny-human rage (which sometimes, I'll admit, was hilariously cute), and then leave floating on a cloud as if homeostasis had been restored. It was that effective. And it had nothing to do with me, and everything to do with the power of art. Of course, I knew this to be true personally, after what I'd just been through senior year. But watching kids experience it at such a young age gave me a whole newfound theory of change.

I was fully convinced this was my calling. I could keep building my education career, influence positive mental health for future generations, AND tap into my artistic side. It was my first post-grad eureka moment. So, I turned down my job offer with Teach for America and looked into Master's Degrees for teaching art. When I found the perfect one, a one-year, highly rigorous Master in Teaching program for K-12 Visual Art at Tufts, in Collaboration with the School of the Museum of Fine Arts (a mouthful, I know), the deadline for submission had passed three weeks prior.

I remembered my Painting 1 experience at that moment. What if I just.. asked? So I did. I emailed the director of the entire program with my best manners in tow. She called me one hour later, and we discussed my application. Luckily, because of Teach for America, all my materials were in order already (transcripts, recommendations, etc.). I was accepted and started classes three months later.

The next challenge was affording it on top of rent. I managed to pay for it myself with scholarship money, a very small loan, and extra income from taking on a paid internship two days a week at the Isabella Stewart Gardner Museum. I knew the Orange Line, Fenway, and the Medford bound bus schedules like the back of my hand. Between school and my internship, I studied and worked six days a week and spent the seventh doing homework, lesson planning for student teaching, applying to real teaching jobs, studying for the MTELs, and maybe doing an errand or two. For the second post-grad year in a row, all I did was work.

The only art I made during this year was via the studio classes I was required to take at Tufts. However, none were painting classes, as it behooved me most as an aspiring art teacher to learn mediums in which I was not yet apt. So, I took courses like ceramics, printmaking, and collage. Although I was creating, I wasn't expressing. There's a big difference there. Unfortunately, the second year of non-expression rolled over into a third. I was hired right out of my Master's program, by Boston Public Schools (the same district that initially inspired me), and I started more or less right away. I was ecstatic but totally blind to my declining mental health.

At 24 years old, I was the youngest teacher with a Master's degree at the James Otis Elementary School in East Boston. I was their one and only Visual Art teacher, which was a dream position to even exist. Not every school has the budget for an art teacher at all, let alone more than one. It was run by hard-core, dedicated, veteran teachers and administrators who taught me all the lessons Tufts could not, and it was filled with the most adorable sponges for learning with all different backgrounds who captured my heart on day one. Today, I like to consider this position my first and last "real job." I was hired in May of 2018, and I resigned in August of 2021. Here's why:

PANDEMIC PLOT TWIST

Hear me loud and clear: I. Loved. That. Job. It was everything I hoped it would be, and so much harder. It was far from perfect, in a 200-year-old building with drastic physical limitations, but it just pushed me to get creative with how to reach my goals, and I got better every day. I taught almost every classroom in the school (about 400 kids) every week, and I knew all their names. I got roughly 50 hugs and 500 "hi Ms. S's" every day, which is average for your typical teacher of tiny humans. I worked my tail off to craft high-quality lessons because of how my students reacted when I did it well.

I saw their eyes light up when I taught them about living, working artists who have skin tones and hair textures just like theirs making fascinating, powerful work. I listened to pure joy and giggles when they experienced new materials and techniques. I watched them play make-believe with their new "friends": Patty Paintbrush & her neat hairdo, Mr. Sharpie & his black top hat, and "Roy G. Biv," a rainbow stick figure man I used as a tool to teach the rainbow order acronym. I saw friendships grow by giving them space to depict their imaginations, express their ideas, and tell stories about their own lives through art. I witnessed empathy flow when children who couldn't speak a lick of English yet managed to communicate through pictures. I had conversations with parents of kindergartners who couldn't believe their child used vocabulary like "primary and secondary colors" at home. I made the "art room" (most of the time this was just me with a box of supplies visiting their classrooms) a safe space for kids who were going through a tough time. That first year one of our kindergartners' mothers died of cancer. I hadn't told any colleagues about my mom, but I told him, and I made it our little secret. He visited me every day that first week, and from time to time throughout the year.

I hit the ground running that first year, happy to dutifully oblige, and I did feel a lot of fulfillment from the job itself. However, I was having a hard time with life after work. I did almost nothing else but teach and plan to do more teaching when I got home. Ask any first-year teacher, (heck, any teacher period) and they'll know this exhausting feeling. So, while I knew this was "normal", by the end of my first year, I was beyond just exhausted; I felt like I didn't know who Katie was anymore. I didn't keep hobbies, barely saw friends, didn't travel much, and truly wasn't very happy at all. I remember feeling like I couldn't afford to spend energy on anything else but my job, so I didn't. But in truth, I did have a lot of free time for the first time in my life. School ended at 3pm after all. I had it, but I didn't know what to do with it, so I either did more work or did "nothing" activities like binging TV. Life after work was hard because I wasn't putting any effort into it. I didn't know how to enjoy it. Or maybe, I didn't think I deserved to.

Looking back, it's clear to me that this was due to two things. First, I wanted to excel so badly at the job I loved so much that I forgot how to take care of myself. The other part, which is harder to admit, is that I also threw myself into work because any time I slowed down or focused on myself, all I felt was heartbreak. I missed my mom, and I hadn't taken much time to grieve her at all since graduating. I was scared to confront the state of my mind and my heart, but it became clear I could only use my job as a distraction until 3pm. I was trying to run from my grief, and it was catching up to me fast. Grief is like a pet elephant. You can only cover it with a blanket, lengthen the leash, and pretend it's not there for so long. Sooner or later you're going to have to confront, tame, and set free that elephant slowing you down on your way to the rest of your life. "You have free time now," I remember telling myself at one point, like a sage speaking to a grasshopper on a foreign topic. I knew I needed to start using it for joy, healing, and grieving. Good thing I knew exactly how to get there. It was clear as day. I needed to paint again.

I knew I wasn't going to get what I needed from my ironing board in the corner. I needed to pick back up where I left off and dive back into my color process with my beloved oil paints and panel boards. To do this, I knew I needed wall space and a room that could stay messy. I needed a studio. Ellie taught me by example how to be a very Frugal Fanny, which came in handy at this point. As long as I spent conservatively elsewhere, I calculated that my second-year teacher salary was enough to invest in renting a real studio of my own. Normal people my age were spending their hard-earned money on concerts, dining out, going to bars, traveling, and trendy clothes. I spent mine on my first studio and art supplies.

I started researching spaces over the summer. The entire process was daunting and "nothing was available." Then, I started networking and asking every artist I knew for advice. It became clear that while SoWa on Washington Street in the South End was the best of the best, it was also the hardest to get into. Three-year waiting list, I was told. I feel like you know what might happen next. This leads me to a small but important digression: If it ever seems a door is closed to you, knock *politely* anyway with a strong elevator pitch at the ready. The worst that can happen is you'll be told no or ignored. Some of the best things in my life had already come to be this way, so I did it again here. I visited SoWa as much as I could and made myself a very squeaky wheel. Channeling my inner

Ellie, I introduced myself to everyone, was kind, and asked tons of questions, including whether anyone was looking to share or sublet space. Sure enough, eventually, two angels named Sharon Shindler and Kim Stockwell answered my call. They said they had others asking, but I was so enthusiastic and polite that they simply liked me best.

This next bit I cannot make up, and I consider it the greatest moment of divine timing in my life so far. I got the keys to that first studio in February 2020. I couldn't have known about the COVID-19 pandemic the same way I couldn't have known what would happen to Mom. But both times, I somehow set myself up to be painting at the most critical timing of both crises.

I think everyone remembers where they were when the news came out that we were officially in a worldwide pandemic. It was Friday, March 13th, 2020, and the pandemic had been announced on Wednesday the 11th. My teacher friends were over at my apartment after we were sent home at the end of the day with the instruction, "Take what you need for at least a few weeks because it's not an 'if' in terms of going remote, it's a 'when' and that timing will be announced tonight." Boston Public Schools announced we were going remote immediately, and set to come back on April 27th. We were shocked and unaware that that would of course change. And so would everything else about teaching our students. Everything changed, in some way, over and over, every day, for the next year and a half. We perpetually had little knowledge about what we were doing, or expected to be doing. But to be fair, I don't think anyone did.

I can barely speak about teaching elementary art through COVID. It truly makes me ill with sadness to recount, because it was indeed traumatizing for all parties involved, especially the students and their families. Instead of 400 smiling faces, I now had 400 portal screens into how the pandemic was playing out in my students' families' homes, if they kept their video on that is. Some days, I spoke into a silent, black screen. It was quite literally like screaming into a void while watching the chaos unfold. Teaching elementary art over Zoom was a bit like leading a thirsty horse to a *picture* of water. It made no sense, and I struggled through every single second of it. Everything I loved about my job, about school in general, all the magic of teaching art, it was nearly lost, dysmorphic at best. I grieved the job I loved; the one I had just started, worked so hard to get, was just getting good at, and that gave me a whole new purpose. In a flash, it turned into a beast I did not recognize at all, and all of us teachers knew nothing would ever be the same.

Of course, all the while I was hyper-aware that people were dying, and how dare I feel sorry for myself while I was alive, employed, and without kids of my own stuck at home with me. I was one of the "lucky ones," but I still had plenty to grieve both personally and collectively as a member of the human race at this moment in time. Just when I was getting used to all my free time, the pandemic compounded it, which meant even more time to think about missing mom, navigating my first devastating breakup, and my teaching job going belly-up. Those personal grievances were layered on top of all the concurrent collective traumas everyone was feeling: the casualties of COVID-19, rampant racism, xenophobia, police brutality, and natural disasters. Not to mention, watching politicians on both sides argue about how to handle these crises in the 2020 election was akin to watching an elementary school food fight. A worldwide mental health crisis unfolded, as it felt like we were all surrounded by catastrophe, misery, darkness, doom, and hatred. We were trapped at home, watching it all on the news, and there wasn't much to cling to for hope.

Fortunately, my new set of keys unlocked the only place I could turn it all off for a moment. I just didn't know that it would set me free.

THE LEAP

In no small way and no dramatic terms, having that studio saved me. Every second I wasn't on Zoom, I was getting back in touch with paint, without the distraction of social plans. Many artists will tell you it was an oddly magical time to create. Finally, our constant desire to hermit crab away from the world, say no to plans, and yes to making art, was granted! Slowly, I could feel my soul coming back to life. I had regained my way to turn off my overworking brain, and instead listen to my emotions, play with color, and discover connections to life. I finally had a chance to hone my emotional intelligence, as the color coaxed the feelings out of me like animals that had burrowed for a long winter, sensing sunshine. Some of those feelings, colors, connections, and discoveries were joyful, exciting, and beautiful. Others were painful, ugly, and scary. But either way, every time, they were better out than in.

It's a dark thing to reframe positively, but there was a flip side to the covid coin, as many people found. It forced unprecedented circumstances that created unexpected growth in gratitude, enlightenment, new perspectives, closeness, innovative connectedness, new hobbies, the sweetness of slowness, and even joy. For me, it created opportunities I otherwise would have never had. It was as if my studio was the Garden of Eden, I was Eve, and forbidden fruit was everywhere. I learned so much, so fast, and I couldn't unlearn it once I knew.

The first thing I learned was also the most important. Painting was so much more than just a hobby. It was undeniably my method of healing, self-care, expression, and joy. I come back to this often when I'm feeling stuck.

Next, because COVID canceled all in-person shows, open studios, etc., the Internet was the only way to show and sell your work, and marketing was paramount. So, while some people learned how to make sourdough, I learned: Instagram for business, website design, SEO optimization, digital portfolio design, video editing, email list building, photography & mockups, staging, automation, e-commerce, and social media networking. Again, there was nothing but time, and I used it to embrace being a beginner with new skills. I did not come anywhere close to mastery (I'm very much still learning today), and by no means did I accomplish this alone. I leaned on my new network of artists and entrepreneurs heavily to grow my knowledge here. And I made a lot of new friends along the way. I am deeply indebted to all the people who responded when I cold DMed them, whose videos I watched, who offered to walk me through new skills, who helped troubleshoot things with me, or who made a masked visit to collaborate. It took a village. And sometimes instead of skill-building we just talked about our roses, buds, and thorns as creatives. Some of these people became very close, lifelong friends. Some of these people were just there for a season of growth. But every single one of them knows how grateful I am, and if you don't, I am here to tell you this book would not exist without you. It's important to mention here that at this point, my only motivation to sell my work was to be able to afford the studio itself, and more materials to make more work (which is frankly still the main reason today). I simply wanted to fund my own healing method. Unexpectedly, 2020 influenced a heightened appreciation for home decor and art. Everyone was stuck at home, slowly getting sick of their walls. Thanks to my new Instagram and website, as early as the summer of 2020, I started getting hired for commissions. Once the first couple were out, they just kept coming. I learned that word-of-mouth marketing is still the ever-reigning king. My hobby quickly morphed into a "jobby." I was so excited to deliver my first commission that I forgot to wire it. The first time someone asked me to install a painting unexpectedly, I didn't know how and I learned on the fly. Mistakes and unpreparedness happened just as frequently as the moments of success. But I learned that that's all part of it. Whatever your goal is, if you wait until you are perfectly ready and know everything, you'll never start.

Perhaps the most powerful of the forbidden fruits was when I first started personally delivering my art. Simply witnessing the joy and uplift on people's faces, because of something I had created now adorning their home, was the best feeling in the world. It was just as magical as teaching an awesome lesson, but with an extra twinge of fulfillment, knowing that their joy would not be confined to that one moment. It would persist once I left, be shared with others, and last through generations. It was mind-boggling to me, the way an object that boosted my wellness to create in the short term could bring others of all ages and stages in life a boost indefinitely. Learning that I had the power to create this difference in people's lives was incredibly empowering, humbling, and completely addicting all at the same time.

When my third year of teaching started, things got... complicated. Teaching became near impossible, balancing both in-person and Zoom instruction (sometimes concurrently), through a mask, 6 feet apart from children used to getting hugs. To no one's surprise, teaching in 2021 was even more demanding and complex than in 2020. It took nearly all of my energy to get through each day and prepare for the next. And then, my jobby needed attention too. Commissions were still coming in, which took priority during my beloved post-zoom studio hours. Although I genuinely enjoyed every single one, after a while I realized that I was spending nearly all my studio time creating other people's visions. I had little time and even less brain space to make my own work, express my own thoughts, and heal in my own way. Even when I didn't have a commission, the exhaustion of the teaching day stifled most of my creative thinking. My grip on my self-care strategy was slipping through my fingers, once again.

You cannot pour from an empty cup. But that's what it felt like I was doing as we approached the end of the school year. I was struggling to bring my best self to my students, which scared me. I was sluggish and disgruntled in the studio, which made me sad. I asked my principal if my position could be adjusted to part-time, but that was uncertain, undesired, and would complicate a delicate balance she deserved to keep at the Otis for the students and staff. I knew something had to give, but I couldn't bear the thought of giving up on my art.

Plus, it wasn't just meaningful to me anymore. I was learning that it meant something to others as well. In late winter of 2021, masked open studios started up again in my building. I met hundreds of new people who turned into followers, friends, collectors, and clients. While in my studio, sometimes without them knowing I was the artist and I was listening, I would hear unforgettable things like:

"Oh this is so happy."

"Wow, it's like, instant calm."

"I didn't know blue could calm me down like that."

"These colors remind me of home."

"How could anyone not feel better after a minute in here?"

"I can't stop smiling."

"It's the best of both worlds, you get joy from the color and calm from the lines."

"This one is me, this is my energy."

"I forget what I was upset about before."

"It's so soothing."

"Look babe, that one's me and this one's you."

"This is the happiest place on earth."

"It feels like a deep breath."

"That one looks like my daughter."

"*sigh*…I needed this."

Of course, these were just the gems that could be put into audible words. Some of my favorite reactions were speechless gasps, gaping smiles, transfixed mindful looking, and the occasional immediate break into a happy dance. This was before I even started writing about each piece. In Spring of 2021, I began sharing brief statements next to each painting. I wrote about what each one felt like, a memory it carried, a lesson it was trying to teach me, or a metaphor it conjured. They spanned lighthearted subjects like the joys of nature as well as honest vulnerabilities on tough subjects like loss.

When I started displaying those next to each piece, eavesdropping gave way to much more meaningful conversations. I was told things like:

"I feel like I have a new way to appreciate abstract art now."

"This describes the way I feel all the time."

"You take the simple, subtle, sweet stuff of life and make them visual."

"Thank you for speaking honestly about that, no one does that."

"I feel completely differently about blue, but I still empathize with this."

"I'm going through something right now and this means a lot to hear."

"If I read that every morning it would change my life."

Two stories stick out to me in particular. One person sent me a message after a show of mine, saying that she sobbed the entire way home in her car in gratitude for my openness and vulnerability about suicide survivorship. She felt seen, full of hope, and not alone. Another woman visited me in the studio to thank me personally. She said after meeting me and following me for a while, she felt brave enough to sit her kids down and reveal that their grandmother, her mother, had lost her life to suicide, not natural causes. It was a family secret she had been keeping for fear of stigma her whole life. She felt free and relieved of a burdensome secret.

Also around this time, two things happened at school. First, somehow one of my colleagues discovered my Instagram and then did a deep dive on my website. She came running up to me at school the next day and whispered, "I had no idea you were so talented.. what on earth are you still doing here?" Another day, I was teaching a lesson on color and decided to share some of my own work instead of a different contemporary artist as a way to connect the lesson to real life. It was part of my curriculum and within my learning goals to teach them that artists are valuable members of society who, yes, can and do make a living by expressing themselves, which adds to our collective understanding of life, history, and culture. I hadn't shared much with them about my art at this point, but I also thought it important to show the kids that artists are also everyday people who are around them all the time. In the middle of the lesson, at a fairly inopportune moment for questions, one of my most inquisitive, thoughtful, curious third graders raised his hand, ferociously. He wasn't even a big fan of art class, but regardless, this came out of his mouth, having understood the lesson a little too well and more deeply than I'd intended:

"Wait... Ms. S, if you're a teacher *and* an artist, why aren't you just an artist? That's, like, so much cooler."

Even in my shock, I'm proud to recount that, without skipping a beat, I answered him with what was and will always be one of my truest truths:

"Because I love being your teacher."

Teachers are professionals in saying what needs to be said while thinking something totally different. So, while I did say that, and while it was honest, my thoughts exactly were "You little wise-alec... you might have a point."

From that moment on, I was in turmoil. Caught between a rock and a hard place, between two careers that had captured my heart and mind, I was terrified to lose any bit of either. And while it's good to love many things, unfortunately, the day is only 24 hours long, and I am someone who puts my whole heart into whatever I do. What hurts the most is that they both deserved it. Regardless, I had a choice to make.

Do I stick with a stable, reliable, but fixed salary? Or, do I take full control of my earnings which are uncertain but unlimited? Do I significantly impact 400 kids a year at school, or potentially reach limitless people of all ages exponentially via shows and social media? Is it better to be surrounded by people each day who I can't befriend outside of work, or work alone every day, but have the chance to make friends throughout my career? Do I keep building on my growing area of expertise, or accept the challenge of being a beginner again? Do I add my own flare to a career many can do, or do I add my own career to the world that only I can do? Can I stand to spend my life asking "what if," or do I take a risk and live my life without regret?

It was mostly other people asking me that last one, and I couldn't ignore it. Even though it was scary, I knew deep down that I deserved to choose joy, control, opportunity, adventure, healing, and creativity. The world had taken so much from me, maybe it was ok to take something for myself and forge my own path. There's a phrase I love that I learned from Gretchen Rubin's book, *The Happiness Project* which is, "When in doubt, choose the bigger life." In her words, "it works because 'big' means different things to different people." For me, it meant being the change I wanted to see in the world. It meant being brave enough to put my joy, passion, & mental health first and figuring out the rest along the way in a world that typically asks you to do the opposite. It meant investing in myself, betting on me, and believing in my art as the most unique and valuable thing I could offer the world. It meant choosing a life bold and vibrant enough to honor my mom's legacy and make her proud.

In short, I think COVID gave me the gift of perspective. I learned who I was supposed to be, or who I had the power to be if I chose to. And, with the support of people who believed in me, I took action. With self-actualized confidence, passion, and purpose, I held my head high as I wrote my resignation letter in August 2021. Was I 100% ready? Maybe not. But like all gymnasts know, sometimes you just have to take that leap and trust your training to land it safely. So, I leaped, quickly before the outside world could scare me back into submission. The window to choose myself was open, and I couldn't risk letting it slip shut.

I submitted my resignation letter in a coffee shop in the north end of Boston. With a sip of black coffee and a tap of the "send" button, I took the biggest risk of my life. I'm still working on the landing, but from that point on, I have been free to fly.

THE LANDING: LIFE AS A FULL-TIME ARTIST

By no means did I stick this leap. Perfect 10s are fun, but you don't learn anything from them. There were, and still are, plenty of stumbles, which is a good thing. After each one, I get better and better. My life now is a constant cycle of learning, trial and error, risk-taking, reflecting, adjusting, and "trying, trying, again." All those skills I built during the pandemic are like muscles that need regular toning. I switched studios twice and I think I finally have it right with this one that's 100% mine here in Bridgeport, Connecticut. I think it's important to mention that just because I can call myself a full-time artist, does not mean that I've "made it." Rather, I "make it" every day, like a bed. There are far more days spent planting and watering than harvesting. Sometimes my efforts reap a bounty, and sometimes I come home empty-handed. It's tough, but I was built for this. My whole life I have been a brazen workhorse who tackles hard things. Gymnastics was hard, student-athlete life was hard, college was hard, grieving mom was (is) hard, City Year was hard, Tufts was hard, and teaching was hard.

Being a full-time artist is bonkers, but, after everything I have been through and learned about myself, it's the exact kind of "hard" that works best for me. It provides what I now know I need in my life. It yields, more than anything else, an abundance of self-understanding, emotional processing, constant new challenges, human connection & love, personal growth, wellness, meaning, memories, legacy, purpose, and joy. Every day, I get closer and closer to my best self, and I have never looked back. Only forward.

Life is always hard. But I think it's about *choosing* your hard.

I don't want to say much about this chapter of my life as a linear story. I feel it's best expressed "between the lines" in the artwork and statements that follow. But I will share some answers to my most frequently asked questions.

What does a typical day look like?

Contrary to what some have asked, no, I do not "just paint all day." Very few days are that blissful, and no two days are the same, which I love. But I would say, my most "normal" day, which doesn't include any events, meetings, shipments, specific project tasks, or time-sensitive busy work, goes something like this: Rise at 6:30/7, NYT puzzles and coffee, exercise, breakfast with a book, head to the studio by 10ish, administrative tasks, client follow ups & Instagram planning until 2:00ish or I can't stand it any longer, something resembling lunch, paint or other creative work on new pieces until 6:30ish, big dinner, Instagram engagements, check in with friends and family, journaling or reading with tea around 10ish, and turn out the light as close to 11 as I can. It rarely goes that well, but that's the structure I shoot for! Any one of those moments can be thrown off, (happily) with an inquiry, an awesome email, a creative idea, a sale, or a really, really nice day that lures me outside. Some of the best things I've done so far in this career have started as happy interruptions.

What has been the biggest learning curve?

Personally: Wearing every hat, and the constant decision-making of when to put them on and take them off. As a one-woman "artrepreneur," I am the artist, marketer, social media strategist, bookkeeper, website manager, photographer & editor, sales rep, shipper, studio assistant, secretary, custodian, and Human Resources (does anyone need an internship!?). I'm also a person trying to balance all that with rest, travel, fun, relationships, and getting enough sleep/exercise/water/vitamins/etc. It's a lot, and some days I just feel like a paralyzed octopus holding a bunch of hats. I have the freedom to do all these things when and how often I want to and I have learned when to be a tortoise and when to be a hare. I've also learned that because my work is about wellness, there's a lot of crossover. For example, taking a long walk is good for me personally, and it helps me process creative ideas, observe inspiring nature, etc. If I take good care of myself, good work follows. In short, freedom is lovely, but it demands 10x the responsibility, discipline, self-understanding, and patience that a more typical career entails.

Business-wise: Constantly adapting to shifts in marketing strategies and ways to reach new clients online. What worked once doesn't always work forever, and you always have to keep learning!

Creatively: Trusting in the seasons. Sometimes I don't make any work of my own (non-commissions or murals) for weeks. I've learned to lean into moments like this and not force anything. After all, this is usually when my brain and body are absorbing and processing what will soon be the basis of my next series of meaningful work.

How do you cope with unsteady income?

Sales can indeed be unpredictable and unpromised. So, I simply work hard with what I can control. I make sure I am always creating new work and sharing it. I network whenever I can and wherever I go, in person and online. I plan my own events, stick to my own deadlines, and communicate with my followers about when it's all happening. I keep things documented and my website up to date. I keep track of who wants to buy paintings now, later, or down the line. I follow up with those prospective clients and collectors, as well as collaborators, designers, liaisons, and partners. I reach out and inquire about dream projects, shows, and press opportunities. I use manifestation, meditation, and wellness activities to control my attitude, energy, and emotions. I speak enthusiastically and joyfully about what I do. I remain open-minded to new opportunities and streams of income. In short, as long as I continue doing good work, politely knocking on doors, keeping good relationships, being prepared, and keeping my mindset right, financially advantageous opportunities always follow. And, when they do I'm diligent with other areas of control. I know my worth in negotiations and make sure I honor the value of my work when closing deals. I'm intentional with saving and only invest in things that will enhance my goals. I keep a hefty safety net of my earnings, and that's what gets me through the slower months.

What's the best and worst thing about being your own boss?

The best part is also the worst part: everything's my fault. Both the wins and the losses. It's exhausting to manage both myself and my work, but it's amazing to be in control. It's very empowering to choose when and where you do your job and life. The best part is in the small things that have allowed me to experience more small joys: drinking my coffee out of a mug in my comfy chair every morning instead of in a Tervis on the train, going outside for a quick walk when it's brilliant out instead of being chained to a Zoom meeting, traveling or visiting loved ones whenever I want. I can shift most of my job tasks to any hour of the day to make room for pertinent or once-in-a-lifetime chances with people I love, and *that* is worth everything. The flip side of that is if I do that too often, my business can suffer. Protecting my studio time is imperative. Balance, balance, balance.

What's the biggest lifestyle shift you've experienced?

I used to run like a jackrabbit, all the time. Go go go, achieve, achieve, achieve. Now, I live for my tortoise moments. My slow mornings, my walks, my "nothing" time where I just brainstorm or let myself feel. I still have hustle when I need it, but I no longer punish myself for being "unproductive". It's luxurious to be more present and mindful with life as it goes by.

What would you say to someone who wants to be an artist?

I would say if you're meant to be an artist, you don't have to choose it. It chooses you. That's what that compulsion to create is! And you don't have to sell anything or make a living from it to call yourself an artist. Read that again. To young artists out there, all you have to do is listen to your body and brain first. Create what interests you despite what anyone says, and you don't have to show it if you don't want to. Feel things deeply (that's usually natural for us). Journal about it. Be unapologetically yourself without sacrificing kindness to all. Never stop creating, and in moments you can't create, consume all the art of others that you can. Make creative friends and hold them close. Being an independent full-time artist is a choice to be a business person *on top* of being an artist. Be prepared for balance, learning, sacrifice, and patience. If this is your path, the three most important things to do right away are to start documenting everything, start an email list, and build your own website. There are plenty of other books to learn the rest!

Above all, don't be like me. Be you, as loudly as possible.

Where are you now?

Today, I live in my own apartment, and work in my own studio in Bridgeport, Connecticut, close to my most beloved friends and family. I feel more empowered to create and pursue new opportunities than ever, having their support right next door to my independent lifestyle. It took an incredible amount of work, sacrifice, letting go, and soldiering through to get here. My independence is my most cherished asset, and I plan to do great big things with it. I started with this book. It wouldn't have been written without the freedom of my own spaces to inwardly retreat, deeply reflect, authentically feel and articulately express. I thank you, dear reader, for your precious attention and time. If I don't yet have the pleasure of knowing you, I hope to soon. You are the kind of person who gives people like me the confidence to live as their authentic selves. You are the reason my work exists and will continue to grow.

My path is just one of the seven billion - everyone has their own. The beauty of life is in the idiosyncrasies we all forge for ourselves, and finding connections and commonalities along the way. That's why I wrote this book. I hope it makes some of you less alone in this journey. I hope some of you feel inspired to find your own way. I hope you fall in love with yourself and with your own life. I hope some of you find more joy in color moving forward, but mostly, I just hope all of you find joy in whatever form you can. I hope you take care of yourself and your loved ones. And lastly, I hope you come to know that this world is better with you - the truest version of you - living loudly in it.

About the Work

ARTIST STATEMENT

"My work harnesses the healing power of color to promote mindfulness, joy, and mental well-being. I am inspired by emotion, memory, nature, and anything that makes me feel healthy. Color is my language, and my meditative process is my self-care. I strive for a harmonious balance of calming minimalism, captivating color complexity, and uplifting vertical line. Once I achieve that, a story or mood can emerge.

I title each painting after it is done. I listen to the story and then decide if it relates more to a memory, a human process, or a vision for the future. The last step of my process involves writing a brief statement, which helps me discover what each painting is truly about. Most viewers also have their own unique associations when engaging with my work. Through this practice, I have found that my work exposes the deeply personal nature of color as it relates to cognition, emotions, personality, and culture.

I hope my paintings serve as uplifting visual aids for mindfulness and intrinsic contemplation. I share them to provide a moment of peace, positivity, and pause for others, as they do for me. Ultimately, my mission is to foster a brighter, mentally healthier future for all. This higher purpose of my work is dedicated to my mother, Ellie. In honor of her, a percentage of all sales are donated to the American Foundation for Suicide Prevention."

WHY COLOR

The reason for my initial draw towards color was elusive to me until I read the Energy chapter of Ingrid Fetell Lee's book, "Joyful" (highly recommend). It was like discovering a beautifully written version of what I knew as truth in my soul.

"From the moment I started studying joy, it was clear that the liveliest places and objects all have one thing in common: bright, vivid, color… Color is energy made visible…a vibrancy that lets us know our surroundings are alive and can help us thrive… It stirs us out of complacency" (Lee, 16 -22).

Simply put, color is evidence of light, light is energy, energy is joyful, and joy is what makes us feel alive. Joy is the bridge between merely surviving and truly thriving. It makes life worth living. In other words, color is life. Given that too many people are dying, my mother included, due to the suffocation of darkness and depression, color is the antidote I'm most interested in, and helps me manifest a future where suicide is a thing of the past.

My job, as I see it, is to manipulate color in a way that harnesses the most possible joy, peace, uplift, and calm, for myself and others. That doesn't mean filling a canvas with as much hot pink as possible; that would be like baking a cookie with 100% sugar. It's all about balance. And while I get much leeway using minimalism and vertical line as supplemental tools, color is the most important because it's the most powerful. This also means it's also the hardest to control. Color is a wily minx to wrangle; it is just as complex and vast in possibility as it is vulnerable and susceptible to many influences of change and presentation. In short, it is a really really hard thing to get right, but the challenge is a great source of joy for me too.

When I do my job well, color becomes the ultimate tool for storytelling, mood alteration, and metaphor. It's complex enough to represent the wide range of experiences involved with being human, and (when controlled well) simple enough to make statements on those experiences quickly and boldly. After all, color is a powerful, direct line to emotion, and I have learned that life is too short to not be direct.

Losing Mom at age 21 was significant, in terms of timing. I was old enough to have a sense of identity, independence, maturity, and self-sufficiency, but young enough to launch myself into an idealistic, zealous pursuit of understanding what creates a healthy life worth living. Finding color was like finding a research method, emotion regulator, flow generator, and personal wellness pillar all in one.

Color makes me feel better, helps me process things, brings me clarity, and allows me to share my discoveries with you, in that order. The more I rinse and repeat that method, the closer I get to answers, manifestation, and hope for change.

A NOTE ON THIS BOOK'S STRUCTURE

On my website, www.katiesouthworthart.com, you will find my work organized chronologically, by series. Each series captures what I learned, felt, or experienced at the time. While each painting in this book is still labeled with the series to which it belongs, this publication is the first and only place I have grouped paintings into topics. In doing so, it highlights the recurring themes I have addressed over time: joy, lessons from nature, adversity, loss, humanness, wellness, personal growth, and love.

There is no need to explore the work in any kind of order. I encourage you to engage with it as you see fit or as you need inspiration-wise. I only ask that each time you browse you embrace the opportunity to relax, take a mindful moment, and enjoy.

Art & Writing

JOY

LESSONS FROM NATURE

ADVERSITY AND LOSS

HUMANNESS AND WELLNESS

PERSONAL GROWTH AND CAREER

LOVE

On Joy

"Over millions of years of evolution, bright color so reliably predicted nourishment, that it became intertwined with joy."

- INGRID FETELL LEE, *Joyful*

COLORJOY

Acrylic and Gold Leaf on Canvas
60 x 102 in
October 2021

Colorjoy Series

ON JOY

To me, color is like an essential food group. A pillar of holistic health. Consuming fully saturated, bright, vivid color on a daily basis has extraordinary power to boost your mood, stimulate your senses, and fuel your zest for a happy healthy life. Afterall, color is proof of life, energy, and light, which are all anitidotes to darkness and depression. My work is my argument for a revitalization of color in this human era of mental heath crisis.

BRIGHT FUTURE

Acrylic on Canvas
36 x 36 in
February 2021

Antichromaphobia Series

ON JOY

There's a tendancy for Western society to avoid bright, vivid color for fear of being seen as childish, unsophisticated, or grotesque (see *Chromophabia* by David Batchelor). But color is proof of life and vibrancy. It's ingrained in our evolution. To intentionally avoid color is to avoid a deeply rooted source of joy and zest for living. Here, at the beginning of the end of the pandemic, and the global mental health crisis it has induced, let us instead indulge in the healing power of color. We all need more instant joy in this moment in history.

BOAT DAY

Oil and Silver Leaf on Panel
36 x 24 in
October 2021

Colorjoy Series

ON JOY

I grew up fishing with my grandfather, early in the mornings, miles off the shores of Martha's Vineyard. Since then, all my life, my favorite summertime thing to do is to be out on the water with friends and family. Every time I see bobbing hulls in a harbor, I think of those trips and long for the next one.

WITH SPRINKLES

Acrylic and Silver Leaf on Canvas
36 x 24 in
October 2021

Colorjoy Series

ON JOY

How can you not smile at something covered in sprinkles? Try even saying it without smiling. Impossible. Simplest thing in the world.. instant joy. Nowadays I always have sprinkles in my pantry, just in case.

LOBSTER SHACK

Oil and Silver Leaf on Panel
24 x 18 in
October 2021

Colorjoy Series

ON JOY

As a lifelong Vineyard person and someone who went to school in Maine, lobster shacks, no matter where I find them, will always bring me a joyful wave of fond nostalgia. I'm particularly partial to bright red ones, of course.

THE JOY WALL

Oil on Panel
87 x 33 in
April–October 2021

Colorjoy Series

ON JOY

There is such joy in abundance. Fields of flowers, leaves on an autumn walk, stars in an open sky, city lights along a midnight skyline, the candy wall in a sweet shop. Perfect opportunities to manifest abundance in your own life.

JOYFUL JOYFUL

Oil & Acrylic on Panel
24 x 24 in
December 2021

Defining Moments Series

ON JOY

In 2021, I chose joy. Over and over again. Mostly through painting. Because, in other areas, it was quite difficult. This change in my work is extremely noticeable, as I gravitated toward brighter, bolder, joyful color, while maintaining my trademark precision and calming compositions. In August, I finally mustered the courage to leave my job, and pursue my art career full time. To live my most joyful life.

MERMAID HAIR

Acrylic on Canvas
60 x 30 in
January 2022

Unseen Light Series

ON JOY

I think Peter and Wendy had a point. Why grow up and lose your childhood sense of whimsy? Maybe they didn't realize that you're allowed to grow up and still love magic, imagination, and play. Life is too short to take it so seriously. It's full of unseen wonders, hidden around corners and barriers that are both real and those that only exist in your mind. But that doesn't mean they don't exist. So, believe in mermaids. Search for unicorns. Hide things from elves. Because magic is joy. And you deserve all forms of joy that this life can offer.

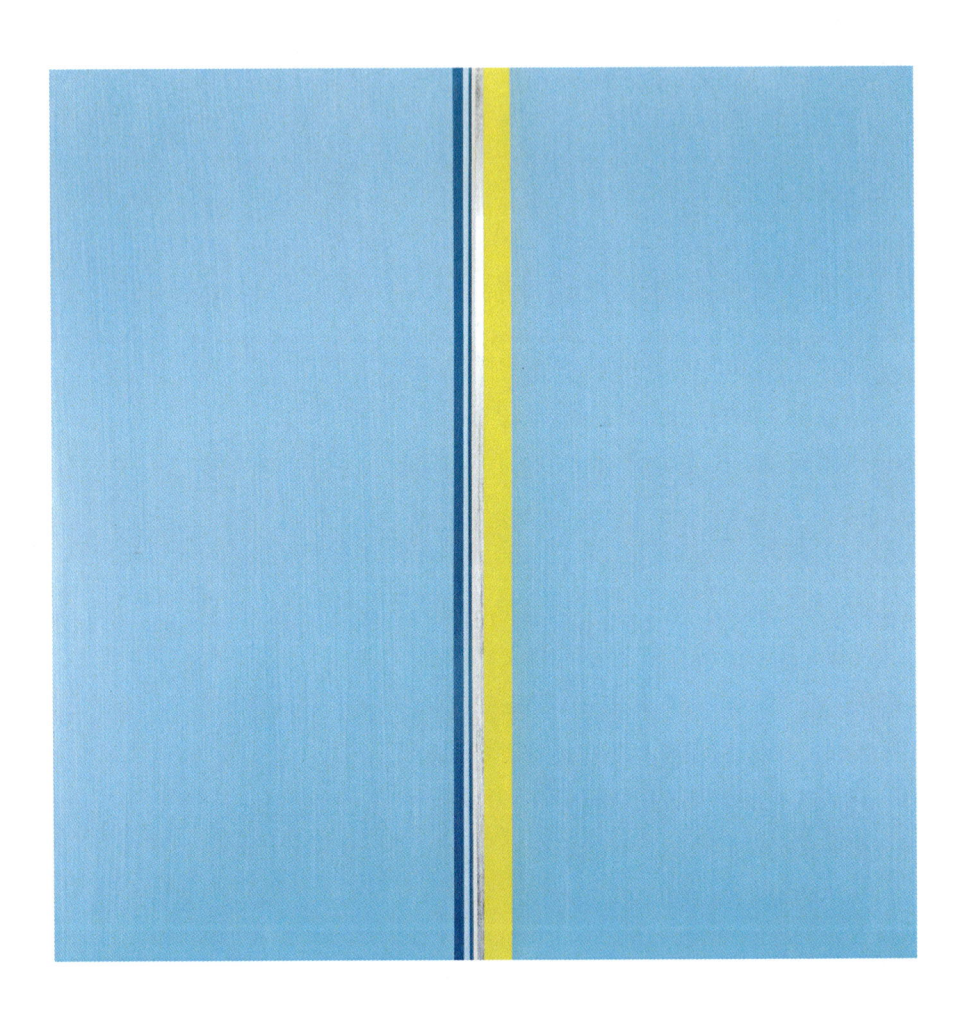

HIGH NOON SAIL

Oil and Silver Leaf on Canvas
30 x 30 in
September 2021

Vineyard Musings Series

ON JOY

The days I'm lucky enough to find myself out on the water, mid day, 75 degrees, clear skies, among friends and family.. they don't compare to anything else. They're what make summer worth waiting for.

ROSE HIPS

Oil on Panel
24 x 18 in
July 2022

Vineyard Musings Series

ON JOY

Among the brightest and most resilient of the roses, Rosa Rugosas typically adorn the greenery leading up to the cape's beaches. Their fruits that bloom after the petals are called rose hips, which have powerful antioxidants and vitamin C, a super food for fighting disease. These flowers are delightfully bright and joyful, but I bet you didnt know they could literally boost your physical health too. Color = joy = health = wellness.

MENEMSHA

Oil on Panel
24 x 30 in
July 2022

Vineyard Musings Series

ON JOY

There's nothing more classic Martha's Vineyard than driving out to Menemsha for a fresh caught lobster to eat with your bare hands, surrounded by tons of colorful fishing junk, right at sunset. It smells of an odd blend of soothing salt and grody fish, but you focus on the delicious fresh cooked food in front of you. I pretty much force this upon any guest of mine who's never been to the island before. I tell them it's for them, but really, it's for me.

WATERMELON SLICE

Oil and Silver Leaf on Panel
24 x 6 in
August 2022

Little Big Things Series

ON JOY

Just as good to look at as it is to eat. The vibrant contrast between outside and inside. The sweetness on your tongue. The jult of refreshing hyrdration. It's happiness in a bite.

SOMEWHERE (OVER THE RAINBOW)

Oil and 3D Mixed Media on Panel
40 x 30 in
October 2022

Transcendence Series

ON JOY

It's difficult to explain in words the joy of watching the Hot Air Balloon Fiesta's mass ascension. Just watching one take off is an overwhelming, sensational phenomenon. The baffling juxtaposition of enormity and "weightlessness". The energizing, giant bulb of color that slowly forms from flat to plump and upright. The secondhand excitement from watching people in tiny baskets being gently lifted into the sky. And finally, the sublime transcendence and freedom of watching it simply float, up, up, and away with the wind, airborne and destined for wherever the muses may take it. Now, multiply all that by 100s over the course of an hour, and try not to have your cheeks aching from smiling. And by the way, it works for kids aged 1 to 100.

TOWEL FOR A GIANT

Acrylic on Canvas
144 x 65 in
September 2022

Transcendence Series

ON JOY

It's always fun to see things on a larger-than-life scale. Including one's own ambitions, dreams, and vision for the future. Which was my intention for this piece. Through a playful, imaginative lens, I see what a giant might take to the beach. Through a psychological lens, I see an overcompensation of joy that I think is missing from the modern human adult experience.

Lessons From Nature

"Come forth into the light of things, let nature be your teacher."

- WILLIAM WORDSWORTH

ON LESSONS FROM NATURE

"Water quiets all of the noise, all the distractions, and connects you to your own thoughts"

- WALLACE J. NICHOLS, *Blue Mind*

Water

PRICELESS

Acrylic and Silver Leaf on Canvas
72 x 24 in
January 2022

Unseen Light Series

ON LESSONS FROM NATURE / WATER

I would choose an ocean view over all the diamonds in the world. I'd pick access to those millions of silver sparkles from the sun over endless silver spoons. The gifts the ocean gives are as abundant as you are there to receive them. And they are priceless.

RIVER

Oil and Tempered Glass on Panel
48 x 12 in
February 2022

Evolve Series

ON LESSONS FROM NATURE / WATER

Recently I found a tiny river off the beaten path of a nature walk, and sat by its side for a while. The rocks both directed the course, as well as interrupted the black depths with glints of magical sparkle. The rest of the world stopped for a minute as I listened to the lullaby of a thing that knew everything and nothing about where it was going. I think our years are like rocks in a river. They might direct our course for the time being but we have no idea where it will lead us next. And that's beautiful.

CHANNEL

Oil and Wampum Shell on Panel
10 x 8 in
August 2023

Sound Mind Series

ON LESSONS FROM NATURE / WATER

Sometimes, the water shows you the way. Following a channel could lead you out of trouble if you're mindful enough to see it. Pay attention to the way life can sometimes show you the way forward instead of trying so hard to figure it out on your own.

STILLNESS

Oil and Wampum Shell on Panel
48 x 12 in
August 2023

Sound Mind Series

ON LESSONS FROM NATURE / WATER

I'll admit I don't like silence very much.
But stillness. I need a bit of that every day.
Stopping to watch the sun sparkle across the
sea, listening to the soft sway of the surf might
be my favorite form.

SHARK!

Oil, 3D Mixed Media, and Mirror on Panel
12 x 12 in
August 2023

Sound Mind Series

ON LESSONS FROM NATURE / WATER

You might be confronted with some frightening things when you're out exploring. That doesn't mean you shouldn't have gone. It means you pushed yourself out of your comfort zone, and you'll probably grow because of it. As long as you don't get eaten!

EBB AND FLOW

Oil, 3D Mixed Media, and Mirror on Panel
40 x 30 in
April 2023

Reflections Series

ON LESSONS FROM NATURE / WATER

Sometimes it's easy to lose sight of ourselves a bit in the highs of life. And it's during the lows when we have to take good, long, honest looks at ourselves, muster up some courage, pick ourselves up, and move forward. It's why many of us retreat to water in times of uncertainty. It's nature's greatest mirror.

ON LESSONS FROM NATURE

"A walk in the woods walks the
soul back home."

- MARY DAVIS

Land

AQUINNAH CLIFFS

Oil on Canvas
30 x 40 in
September 2021

Colorjoy Series

ON LESSONS FROM NATURE / LAND

When covid first hit, I spent a long time quarantining on Martha's Vineyard. There was nothing but time to take long walks exploring corners of the island I'd never been to (despite 27 years of trips). I most enjoyed the time I spent looking closely at the colors of the iconic cliffs. I felt inspired, grounded, and so incredibly grateful that covid couldn't cancel the gift of going outside.

KEEP OFF THE DUNES

Oil on Panel
24 x 30 in
July 2022

Vineyard Musings Series

ON LESSONS FROM NATURE / LAND

Rules: annoying, when you're a child with incessant curiosity, but necessary and worthy of gratitude when you're an adult that appreciates the conservation of the island's natural beauty more than anything.

BLOOM

Oil and Gold Leaf on Panel
96 x 7 in
August 2022

Little Big Things Series

ON LESSONS FROM NATURE / LAND

It's the reach for me. Flowers will always delight with their playful shapes, energetic colors, and resilient growth. I appreciate them for reminding me to keep my focus up toward the golden sun. Stretching for the bloom, toward full self actualization.

CACTUS PATCH

Oil on Panel
30 x 40 in
October 2022

Transcendence Series

ON LESSONS FROM NATURE / LAND

I'm still trying to figure out why I'm so obsessed with cacti. It might have something to do with the extra sense of refreshment and vitality they symbolize, being so green in typically arid environments. Or it could be the way they paint the perfect picture of emotion, being both prickly and pretty at the same time. Or it could be the adorably amorphous, unique shapes they form, which seem delightfully improbable and thus perpetually magical to come across.

BEACH TREASURES

Oil and Glass Bead on Panel
24 x 18 in
July 2022

Vineyard Musings Series

As a child, I would come home from the beach with bag-fulls of shells. Walks at the water's edge with me would take eons, as I stopped to collect every twinkling treasure and sensual scallop. Today, it's more of a visual mindfulness adventure, as I continue to enjoy the glistening interruptions to the sand's darkening gradient towards the sea. And I still pick up the occasional gem. It's the perfect restorative summer activity, with the dull roar of the waves, the cool sand on bare feet, and the nourishing salt in the breeze.

TIGER LILY

Oil and Tempered Glass on Panel
24 x 24 in
April 2023

Reflections Series

ON LESSONS FROM NATURE / LAND

Never forget, beautiful human, that you have
a fierce, brazen, fiery, spirit somewhere within
you. Like a roaring, summer-born tiger lily, face
toward the sun, open, wild, and free.

IT'S NOT EASY

Oil, 3D Mixed Media, and Mirror on Panel
24 x 18 in
May 2023

Reflections Series

ON LESSONS FROM NATURE / LAND

Being green. Being new. Starting fresh. Starting over. Trying something for the first time. Emerging into uncharted territory. Showing up after a while. Scary! But if tiny buds on a branch can do it every spring, so can you.

ON LESSONS FROM NATURE

"Even when everything was falling apart around me, the sky was always there for me"

- YOKO ONO

Sky

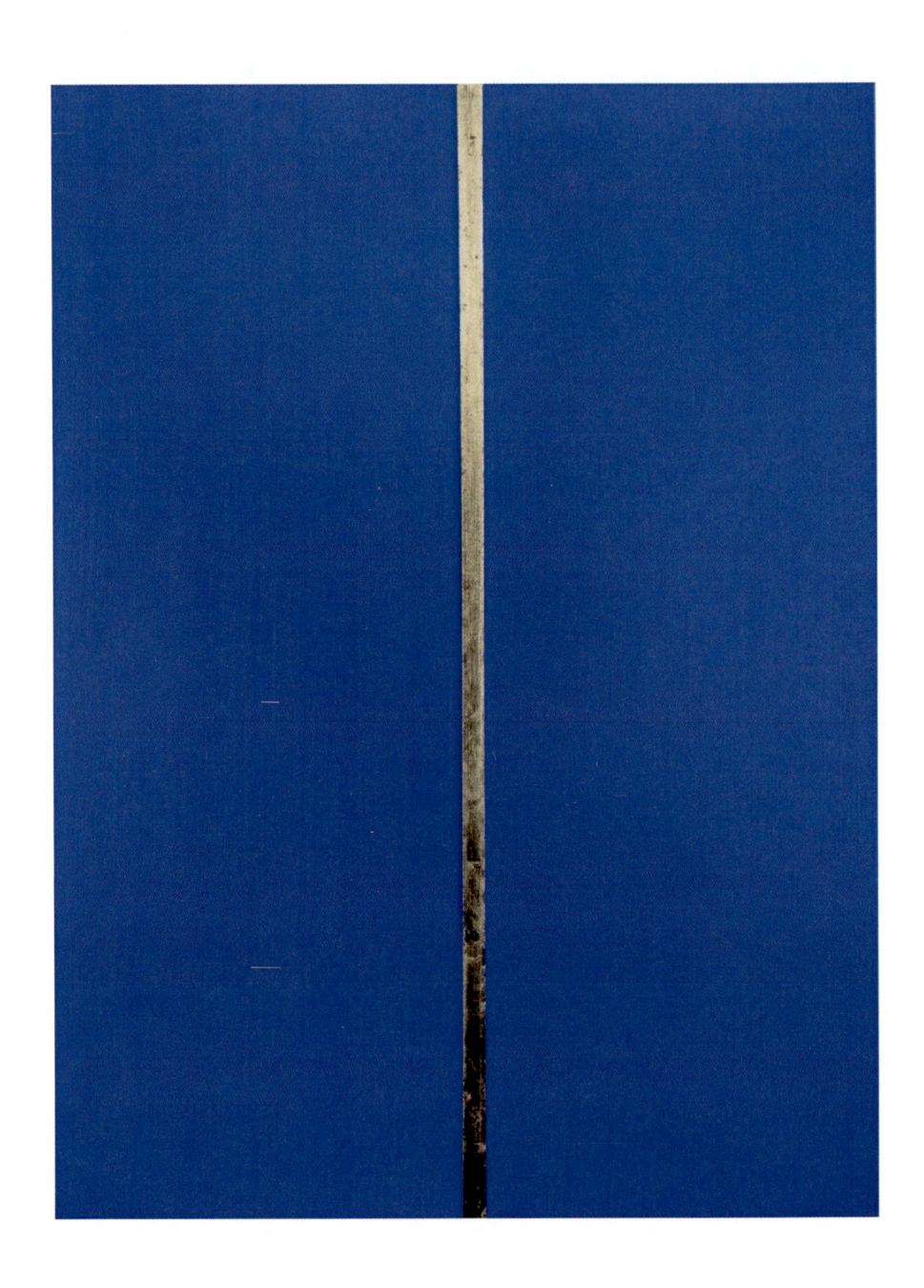

MOONGLOW

Oil and Gold Leaf on Panel
40 x 30 in
August 2021

Colorjoy Series

ON LESSONS FROM NATURE / SKY

So sublime is the sparkle of the moon on the water. Her mysterious wisdom from trips around the earth calls to us with a glow soft enough at which to stare. The vastness of the sea reflects her light in service of compounding her power. Awestruck, we listen and learn the lessons we already know inside us, waiting to be realized.

GOLDEN HOUR

Oil and 3D Mixed Media on Panel
24 x 18 in
June 2022

Emergence Series

ON LESSONS FROM NATURE / SKY

Golden hour is more than just a perfect photo-op. It's a little magic we're spoiled with, everyday. A visual cue to consider the beauty of life, say thank you, and look forward to tomorrow.

EL SOL

Oil and Gold Leaf on Panel
24 x 24 in
September 2021

Colorjoy Series

ON LESSONS FROM NATURE / SKY

All my favorite Vineyard activities depend on sunshine. "Clear skies" practically equates to "fun day". But we need the rain to keep the sunny days special. So this painting is for those like me who might need some bright yellow sunshine energy on those unavoidable rainy days. It's the same reason my rain jacket is yellow.

MOONRISE

Oil, 3D Mixed Media, and Gold Leaf on Panel
36 x 24 in
August 2022

Little Big Things Series

ON LESSONS FROM NATURE / SKY

I've been returning to the same spot to watch summer sunsets for 28 years. Mostly for the 360 viewpoint, because for me, the duality of it is important. Most people watch the dance of the deep pinks and oranges of the setting sun. I like to pay equal attention to the other side of the sky, where pale blue darkens to indigo, painting a perfect path for the rising moon, as she takes her place for the night. Be grateful for the quiet side of things, you need it to keep the flashy thrills special.

OPEN AIR

Oil on Panel
18 x 24 in
October 2022

Transcendence Series

ON LESSONS FROM NATURE / SKY

Leave it to a large, clear sky to open your mind, broaden your perspective, and lift the weight of your worries. The simple upturn of your chin is enough to boost serotonin. The wide cerulean expanse calms the nerves as your mind wanders as far as the atmosphere inspires.

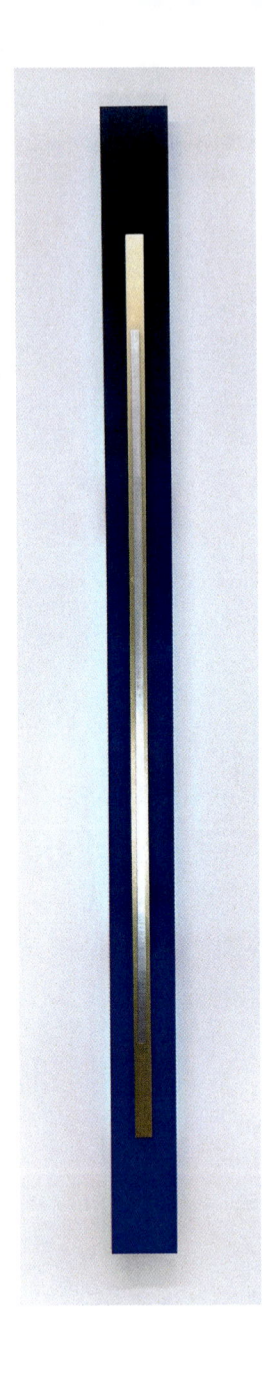

LUNA

Oil, 3D Mixed Media, and LED on Panel
96 x 5.5 in
February 2023

Evolve Series

ON LESSONS FROM NATURE / SKY

On birthdays it's typical to reflect on another "trip around the sun" and celebrate the beginning of a new one. As a night owl, I do some of my best thinking, writing, and creating by the light of the moon. Not only that, she is a powerful and reliable teacher in patience, braving phases, and trusting in the cyclical nature of things. Today, 2/14/23, I'm looking forward to my 29th year of lunar lessons.

On Adversity & Loss

"If you are uncomfortable—in deep pain, angry, yearning, confused—you don't have a problem, you have a life."

- GLENNON DOYLE, *Untamed*

MONARCH MOMENTS

Oil on Panel
24 x 36 in
October 2021

Colorjoy Series

ON LOSS & ADVERSITY

Since losing my mom, I've become a lot more in touch with my spiritual side. I truly do feel her energy, love, and warmth whenever a monarch flutters by. And I have found that they seem to pop by in big moments when I'm nervous, scared, or doubting myself. I've been lucky to come across plenty of orange ones, and I'm hopeful that someday I'll be graced by a beautiful blue one.

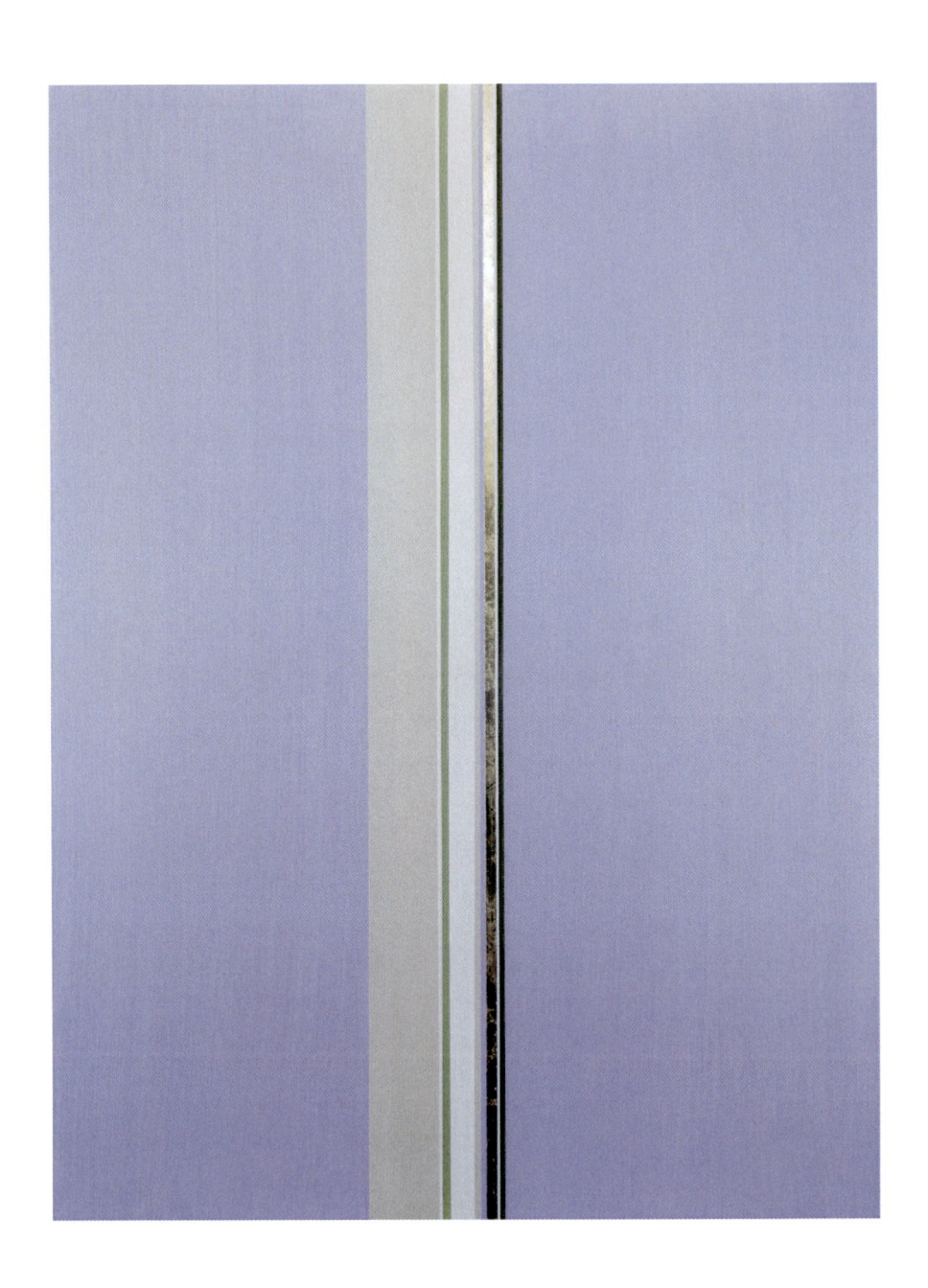

WEEPING WISTERIA

Oil and Gold Leaf on Panel
40 x 30 in
September 2021

Colorjoy Series

ON LOSS & ADVERSITY

When I first met Marc, we connected immediately. We laughed, we cried. Our stories are painted with the same saddening stroke of loss due to suicide. He showed me a painting of his he made to help himself cope. This painting is inspired by that painting. This painting is for Jessica.

Rest in peace, beautiful girl.

BERMUDA SEABREEZE

Oil and Gold Leaf on Panel
24 x 18 in
October 2021

Colorjoy Series

ON LOSS & ADVERSITY

My mom's favorite colors were pink and tangerine orange. Which makes perfect sense to me. She was fun, silly, warm, and, on her good days, a ball of boundless energy and light. I think it's ironic but fitting that her go-to cocktail was a seabreeze: vodka citron with grapefruit and orange. She always politely asked for it with a lemon, and was nearly always given a lime. This one's for her, with a touch of yellow for her lemon. Cheers to you, Mama.

RISE

Acrylic on Canvas
60 x 20 in
January 2022

Unseen Light Series

ON LOSS & ADVERSITY

These past two years, we've all been burned, in one way or the other, in varying degrees, severity, and directness. My form of rising is in creating. I create art, but also, and more importantly, better versions of myself, which sometimes means letting past versions go. So, whether the flames are external or internal, there will always be ashes from which to rise. Thus, there is beauty in the burn. It's when we may begin again, anew.

RETROGRADE

Acrylic on Canvas
60 x 48 in
April 2022

Divergence Series

ON LOSS & ADVERSITY

Sometimes it feels like everything is messed up because of that one person being gone. Sometime's it is. But switching your phrasing from "messed up" to "different now" is a game changer in terms of growing in your ability to thrive against it all.

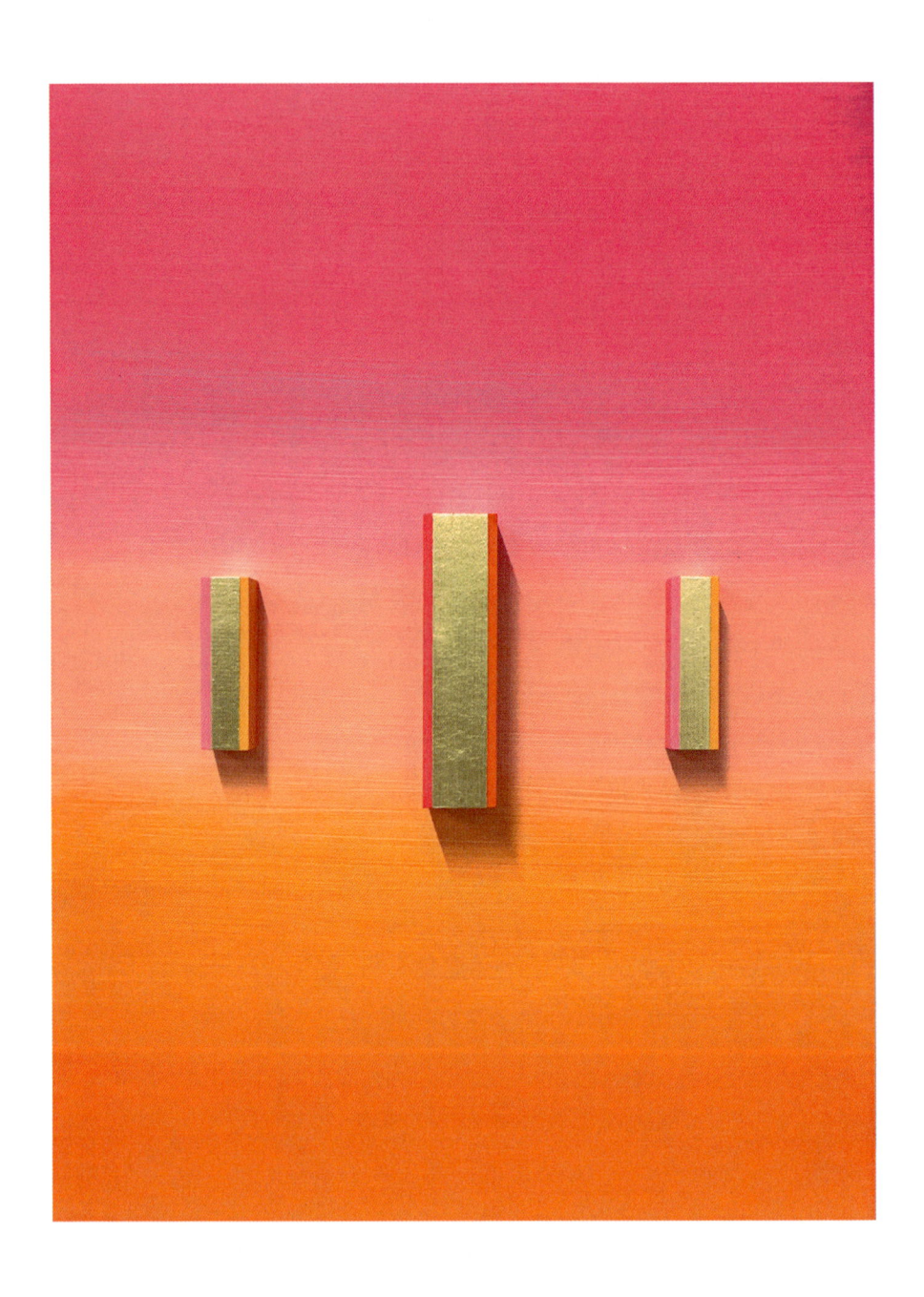

LAST LIGHT

Oil, 3D Mixed Media, and Gold Leaf on Panel
24 x 18 in
August 2022

Little Big Things Series

ON LOSS & ADVERSITY

Is it me, or, when you miss someone who is gone, does the last light of a beautiful day harbor a uniquely profound sadness within its beauty?

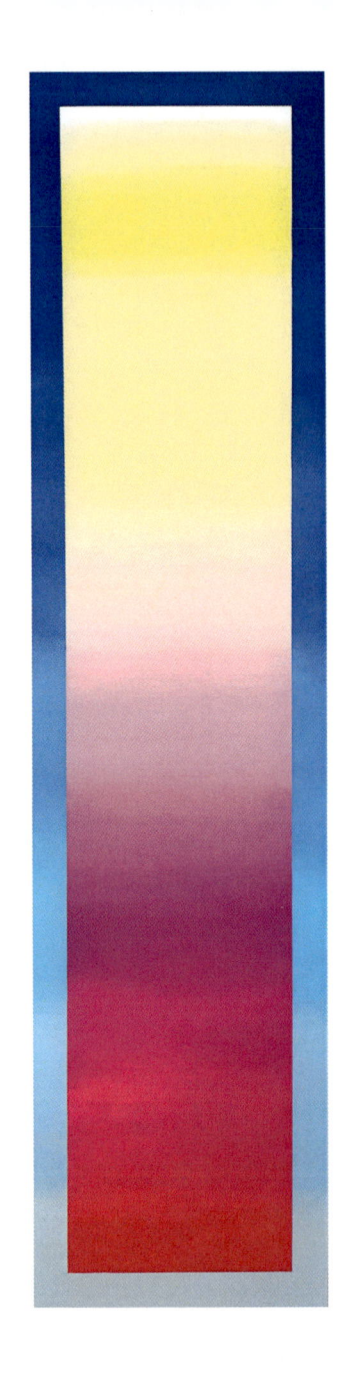

INNER GLOW

Oil on Panel
48 x 12 in
Febuary 2023

Evolve Series

ON LOSS & ADVERSITY

As an ambitious woman who chases big goals, I've experienced my fair share of rejection, disrespect, coldness, and belittlement. At times, I feel surrounded by it and it can be all consuming. But honestly, it's all part of the game. People will underestimate you, and if you're not getting rejected you're not trying hard enough. The key, I've found, is to remember that nothing can dim my inner glow without my permission. And in fact, most of the time the shade actually makes it shine brighter.

BEAUTIFULLY BROKEN

Oil and Tempered Glass on Panel
48 x 24 in
Febuary 2023

Evolve Series

ON LOSS & ADVERSITY

Life will give you plenty of lemons. Some will just be sour for a while, and some will cripple you with everlasting grief. Here's the thing about a shattered heart though: It allows you to let light in and out in more ways than you thought possible. Others who've loved and lost as well will see themselves in you, and you them. There is resilience in togetherness. And the truth is, we are all a little broken.

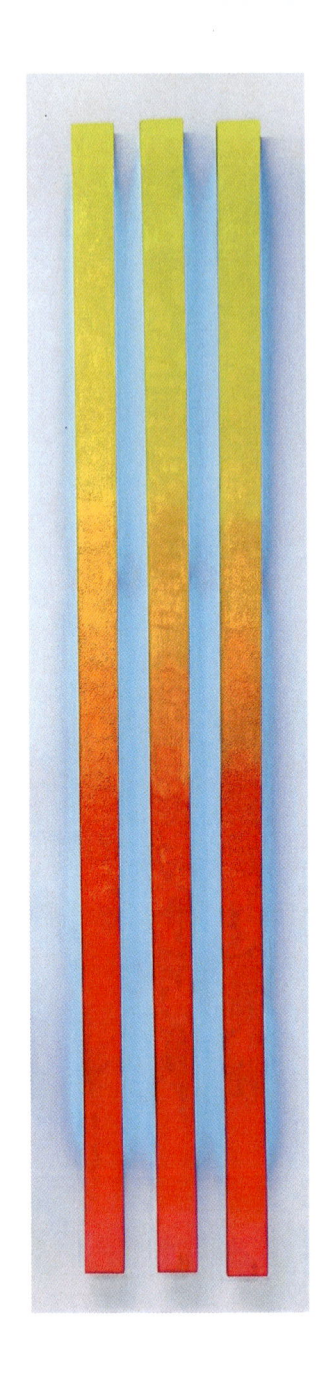

ILLUMINATE

Oil, Sand, and LED on Panel
96 x 18 in
January 2023

Evolve Series

ON LOSS & ADVERSITY

Through Dumbledore, RJK Rowling said it best: "happiness can be found in even the darkest of places, if only one remembers to turn on the light." Most of my work is about using color as a bright spot to drown out darkness. This time, for the first time, I used literal light both to enhance the experience of the color, as well as to function as a halo when the darkness of night takes the color out of vision. The halo is proof that, although I can't see it right now, the color is still very much there, and will be visible when the sun comes up. So, not to worry. Growing older comes with its dark moments. We lose everything from youthful innocence to real people who shaped us as beings. But do we really lose them, or do we just need to remember to illuminate the bits and pieces of them that are very much there, and left within us?

NOT FORGOTTEN

Acrylic and Oil Scrap on Panel
12 x 12 in
Febuary 2023

Evolve Series

ON LOSS & ADVERSITY

What do we do with old stuff? Stuff that's "no longer relevant" from past lives, old relationships, past apartments, early ideas, retired beliefs, old feelings, etc. Do we forget about them? Toss them? Or do they have fascinating histories that represent our choices, our touch, our movements, our thought patterns? I'm not advocating for hoarding, I'm just saying: stuff from our past isn't worthless junk. It carries memories, and histories, and provides proof of a process that led you to where you are today.

TRANSIENT

Oil and Acrylic on Panel
48 x 36 in
January 2023

Evolve Series

ON LOSS & ADVERSITY

One of the hard truths of growing up is realizing that nothing, (absolutely nothing), lasts forever. And even harder, we never get to know how long we have with each person, place, idea, style, thing, whatever it is, before it's gone. This piece, for example, showed me that my process had outgrown the technique behind the style I started with. I was forced to pivot to another process about a quarter of the way through that served my interests and needs a lot better. In other words, I had to do another thing we all struggle with: I had to let go.

PRESENCE OF ABSENCE

Acrylic on Canvas
60x80 in
May 2023

Mother's Day Series

ON LOSS & ADVERSITY

I usually spend Mother's Day by myself, painting. This year, I spent a long time looking at this piece, stuck. I kept thinking, "it's not done, it's incomplete, it needs something, it's missing something". And that's when I realized it was done. It represented exactly how I was feeling. I was missing someone. The painting was like me: A person who is permanently incomplete. My mother's absence is as permanent as it is salient in my life. Without her I will never be whole, but nonetheless I am still alive, full of her beautiful spirit, and capable of participating in this beautiful life.

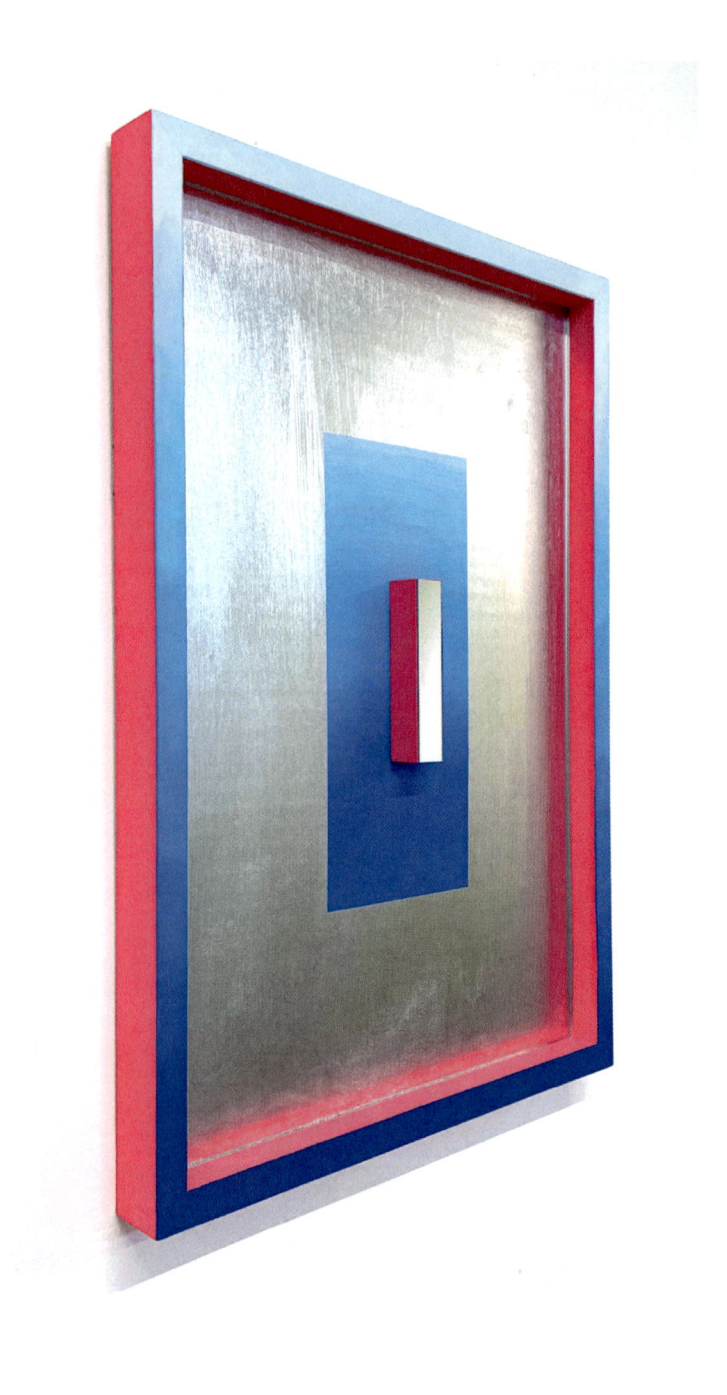

NOT ALONE

Oil, 3D Mixed Media, and Mirror on Panel
24 x 18 in
May 2023

Reflections Series

ON LOSS & ADVERSITY

Our minds can be our worst enemy, and our greatest savior. When you're in the middle of things, that's the worst. Mid-life, mid-crisis, mid-marathon, mid-transition, mid-break-up, middle school (woof), whatever it is. It's easy to feel alone and surrounded by nothing by saddening, ambiguous barriers with no way out. But the power of a change in perspective can't be understated. You might find you are surrounded by all the love, warmth, and support you need to carry on and be ok. Look inward too and you might find the love and warmth you need also resides within you. It always has.

SILVER LININGS

Acrylic, Mixed Metal Leaf, and Mirror on Panel
18 x 24 in
May 2023

Reflections Series

ON LOSS & ADVERSITY

Never underestimate the benefit of looking for the silver linings in tricky situations. You don't have to take the lemons as they are. This painting started out looking very different. I tried a new technique that didn't work out at all, and I hated it. After a long break, I decided to see it as an opportunity and I took it in a completely different direction. I wound up loving the result a whole lot more than the original plan. Just goes to show: often the silver lining is more powerful than the adversity.

FEEL YOUR FEELINGS

Mixed Media on Canvas
120 x 65 in
December 2022

ON LOSS & ADVERSITY

Life, from time to time, gets really really messy. And when we're going through those times, there's a lot of pressure to continue showing up as our best selves. Pressure to be positive, put together, people pleasing. It's the birthplace of "I'm fine". Either that or we hide away, pretend we've "been busy" and quit for a while, hoping to muddle through. But it's ok not to be ok. It's more human to admit you're not ok than to carry on with a fake front that you are. With vulnerability, we receive the love and support that we need to make it through. There's so much help available to all of us. But to receive it you have to be honest about your feelings. Feel them. Name them. Communicate them. Let them come out instead of being ashamed of them and keeping them inside. It doesn't mean you're weak, it means you are alive and participating in this complicated thing called life. So, please, for yourself, for your loved ones, and for all of us, feel your feelings. I usually paint when I feel good. But I for this painting I felt awful, and decided to make something anyway.

ON TIME

Oil, 3D Mixed Media, and Silver Leaf on Panel
24 x 18 in
August 2023

Sound Mind Series 144

ON LOSS & ADVERSITY

Timing is everything, so they say. Sometimes two people aren't meant to be together. Sometimes the relationship works better if both function independently, always knowing where the other is, working in tandem but apart, like two ferry boats passing in the night.

On Humanness & Wellness

"Wellness is the freedom to move fluidly though the cycles of being human. Wellnes is thus not a state of being; it is a state of action."

- EMILY NAGOSKI, *Burnout*

SEQUENCE

Acrylic on Canvas
65 x 120 in
April 2022

Divergence Series

ON HUMANNESS & WELLNESS

Painted one hue at a time, from left to right, this piece is my ode to all human sequences: of emotions, thoughts, or days of our lives. No two colors are the same, but all are connected and inspired by one another. Together, its' a complete harmonious experience made up of various unique component parts.

CLARITY

Acrylic on Canvas
65 x 122 in
March 2022

Flocean Series

ON HUMANNESS & WELLNESS

My deep love and gratitude for the ocean is both personal and profoundly human at the same time. Spending time near water is an incredible catalyst to achieve a state of flow, in which clear-minded decisions, creativity, and inner peace are all achievable. When made into a habit, the blue depths will ease your mind, heal your soul, and, ultimately, help you achieve clarity.

COMMON GROUND

Oil and Vinyl on Panel
40 x 30 in
April 2022

1 of 1

ON HUMANNESS & WELLNESS

How to find common ground in conflict can be daunting. I have found that a good place to start is coming together and noticing commonalities first. Whether noticeable at first glance or not, they're there. Then stepping into the world you don't yet understand, as far as you are able, has to come next. Making amends peacefully is possible with empathy. When all else fails, remember we all share this blue and green planet as home. And we are all 99% the same. Though our differences should always be respected as what makes us beautiful, humanity transcends them all.

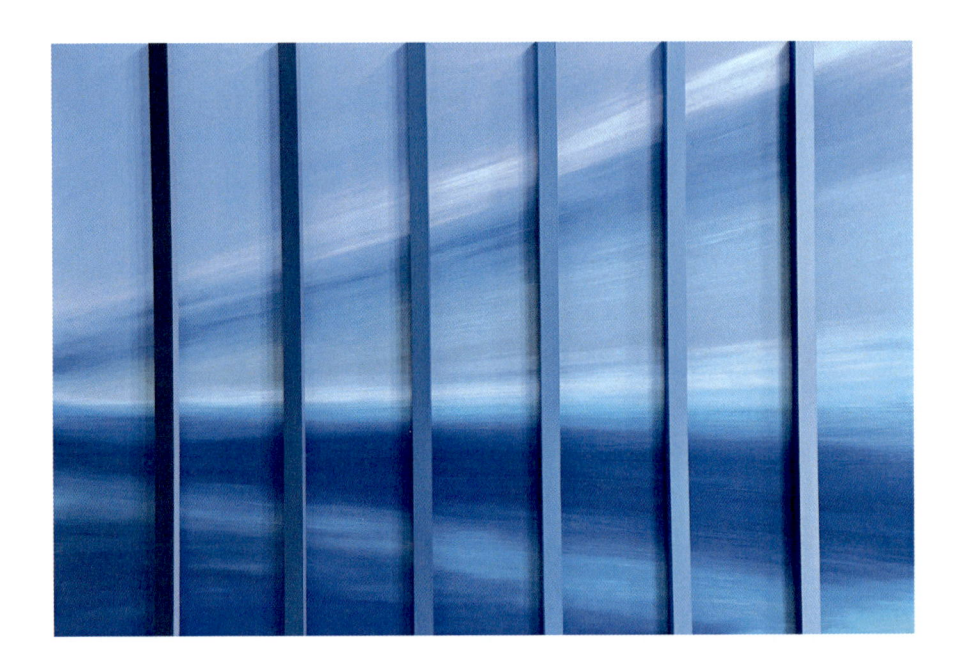

SWELL

Oil, 3D Mixed Media, and Mirror on Panel
24 x 36 in
June 2021

Emergence Series

ON HUMANNESS & WELLNESS

Life has ups and downs, ebbs and flows, storms and smooth sailing. We all know this. And knowing this natural cycle is both a blessing and a curse. But, I think life is less about focusing on the next high or low and more about just enjoying the ride. Being present. Feeling the entire spectrum of life's emotions. Highs, lows, and everything in between. That is being human.

WORK WEEK

Oil, 3D Mixed Media, and Silver Leaf on Panel
24 x 38 in
June 2022

Emergence Series

ON HUMANNESS & WELLNESS

M, T, W, TH, F. We all go through it. Whether you have a 9-5 or are self employed, Monday through Friday is an inescapable bracket of to-do's, deadlines, goals, appointments, and other time sensitive events. Every day is colored by different things, but time has a funny way of blending them all together. Taking each day as it comes is healthy, but so is noticing the trends and commonalities between them all through reflection.

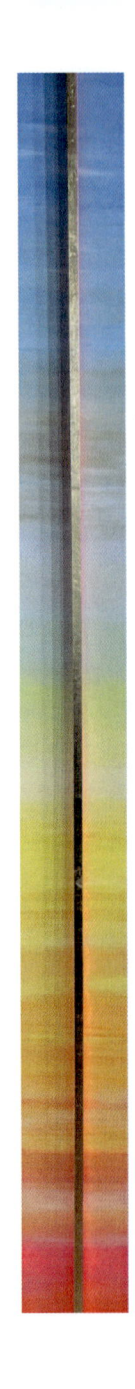

SUN SALUTATION

Oil, 3D Mixed Media, and Gold Leaf on Panel
96 x 9.25 in
June 2022

Emergence Series

ON HUMANNESS & WELLNESS

We spend so much of our days physically looking down whether it be at devices, tasks, chores, dependent family, etc. And that's not necessarily bad. What's problematic is the lack of effort we give to balance that out by focusing our gaze upward. Toward the sun. Lifting your chin boosts serotonin and relieves stress on your neck. This is one of the best gifts from yoga practice. The power of daily sun salutations is not to be underestimated. The extreme verticality of this piece is intentional for this reason, and reminds us of our universal focal point: the sun.

PRANA

Oil, 3D Mixed Media, and Gold Leaf on Panel
24 x 18 in
June 2022

Emergence Series

ON HUMANNESS & WELLNESS

Prana is a Sanskrit word for breath or "life force". It is the nourishing energy we circulate through our bodies. The pulsating background of this piece, the peaks emphasized by golden bars, is meant to visually represent prana - our life sustaining, repetitive pattern of inhales and exhales. Remember that wherever you are in your day, you can always reset and start over. Just take a deep breath, feel the life force surge within you, tell yourself "I am here" and carry on.

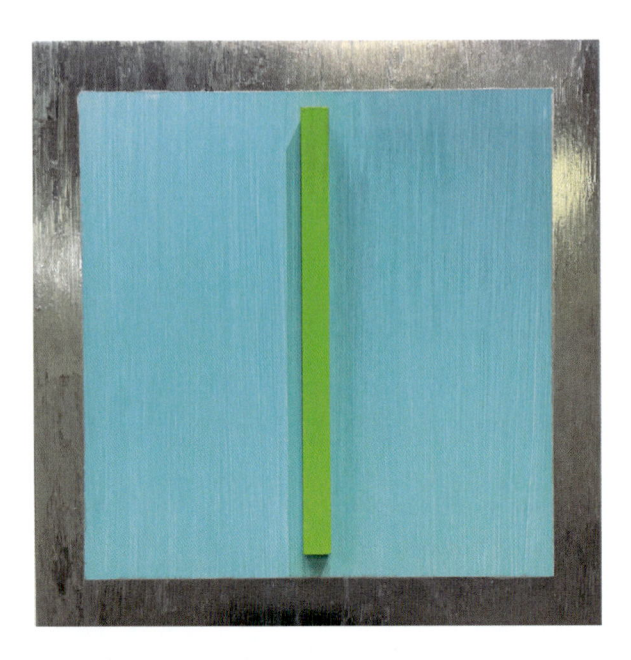

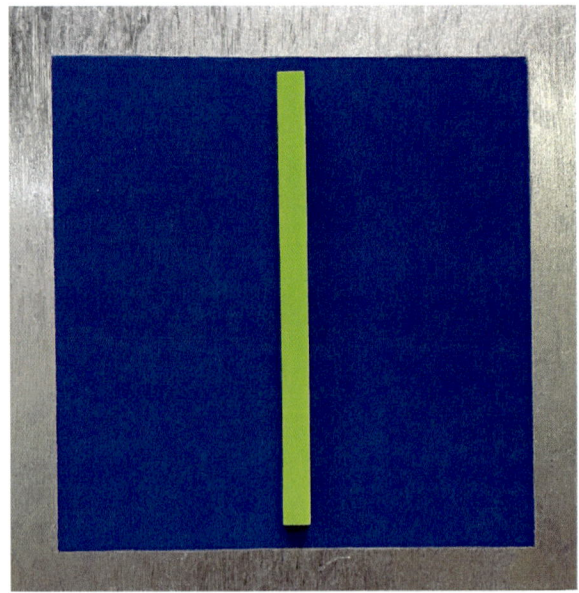

SAME, SAME, BUT DIFFERENT

Oil, 3D Mixed Media, and Mirror Paint on Panel
28 x 12 in
June 2022

Emergence Series

ON HUMANNESS & WELLNESS

Colors are just like people. They present differently depending on their surroundings. In this piece, all instances of green are the same exact hue. I promise. The two different blue environments allow different elements of the same green to shine. This piece was made to encourage you to make note of how you feel and behave in different places, with different groups of people, and in different work environments. This way, you can make more informed decisions on how to feel more like the lower green - bright, strong, & glowing - when you want to, and more like the upper green - calm, comfortable, and quiet - when you need that.

PULSE

Oil and 3D Mixed Media on Panel
24 x 18 in
August 2022

Little Big Things Series

ON HUMANNESS & WELLNESS

Every living thing follows rhythms. We rely on them, physiological and experiential, to carry on. Peaks follow valleys, rainbows after rain, joy replacing sorrow. Exhales. Inhales. Heartbeats. The pulse lets you know you're alive.

FULL HARBOR

Oil, 3D Mixed Media, and Silver Leaf on Panel
36 x 24 in
August 2022

Little Big Things Series

ON HUMANNESS & WELLNESS

Gathering is a human need. Seeing all the moorings slowly fill up at the beginning of summer is proof of people, here to have fun. It reminds me of the joy of getting a group togeher. Like seeing all your friends on the first day of school, arriving to the party to see all your loved ones, or coming home to a full house. A full harbor says "we're here, let's get together."

SONGLINES

Oil and Acrylic on Panel
48 x 36 in
September 2022

Transcendence Series

ON HUMANNESS & WELLNESS

At Colby, every graduating class sits for a "last lecture" from a student selected professor. At mine, among other points of life advice, the lecturer encouraged each of us to "follow your song-line", essentially meaning: follow your own unique path in life while being true to the rhymes and rhythms that come your way, and you'll find the people you're supposed to meet, and do the things your supposed to do. Sometimes, when I look up at the sky at dusk, intersecting, colorful jet streams remind me of those "chance" encounters and special moments that were always destined to be part of one's story. The way my brother met his wife proved this to me.

UP, UP, AND AWAY

Oil and 3D Mixed Media on Panel
40 x 30 in
October 2022

Transcendence Series

ON HUMANNESS & WELLNESS

Something I learned from watching 100s of giant hot air balloons lift off and drift into the distance in whatever direction the wind was gently blowing: Most of what happens to us in this life is out of our control. Not only that, whatever seems huge to you right now, give it time, and it will fade from your mind and life, becoming less and less noticable as time goes by. That could be a good thing or a bad things, but it'll happen either way.

FIRST CROCUS

Oil, 3D Mixed Media, and Mirror on Panel
40 x 30 in
April 2023

Reflections Series

ON HUMANNESS & WELLNESS

One of my biggest smiles of the year comes with the sighting of the first crocus. That perennial signal of spring, renewal, new life, new beginnings, and resilience. The awe of witnessing its ability to bloom forth from the frigid winter ground will never get old. That resilience is reflected in all of us. Nothing is more human than braving the cold winters of adversity and springing forward, regardless.

CITY NEON

Oil and 3D Mixed Media on Panel
30 x 40 in
April 2023

Reflections Series

ON HUMANNESS & WELLNESS

I think there's a lesson to be learned from city neon. Think about it: It's job is to stick out and say "I am here, notice me, please come in". To make itself known when it would otherwise be engulfed, bypassed, and forgotten about in the darkness. Most of all, it welcomes people in, who otherwise wouldn't know they were needed. Vulnerability is neon. It lets people know you need them.

DOCKED

Oil and 3D Mixed Media on Panel
24 x 18 in
August 2023

Sound Mind Series

ON HUMANNESS & WELLNESS

Fortunate is the person who knows that
feeling of coming home. Having a safe place
to continuously return to. It could be anything.
A house, a person, a pylon. Everyone needs a
dock. A place to ride out the storms.

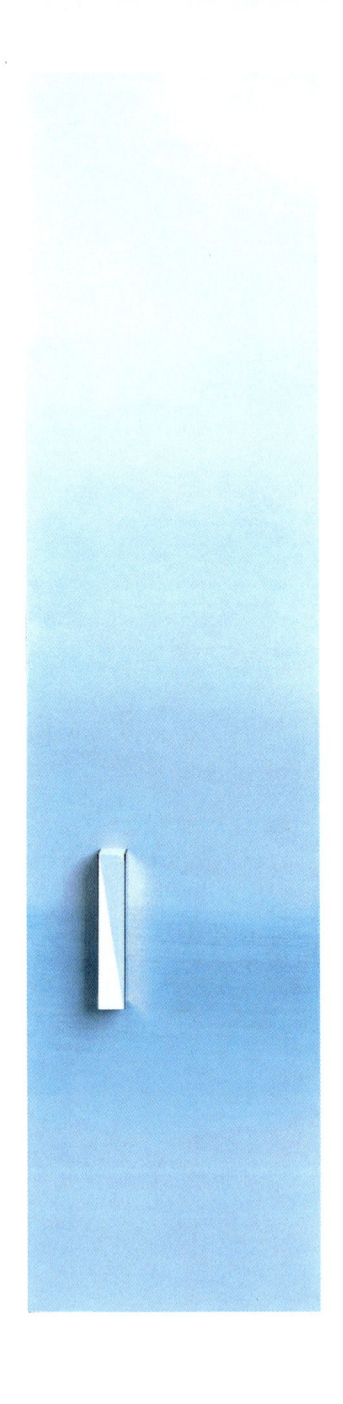

SOLITUDE

Oil, 3D Mixed Media, and Mirror on Panel
48 x 12 in
August 2023

Sound Mind Series

I think embracing alone time is key to reaching a higher self. I'm learning that designating uninterrupted "nothing" time on my own can sometimes be the most productive thing I do that day. It's where ideas are processed and formed. Where learning solidifies. Where mindfulness is welcome, and gratitude can flow. All of this informs my work like nothing else.

REGATTA

Oil, 3D Mixed Media, and Mirror on Panel
24 x 38 in
June 2022

Emergence Series

ON HUMANNESS & WELLNESS

Hoisting a spinnaker and sailing full speed ahead is commendable and all. But life isn't a race. Even if we are forced against the clock a lot of the time. I think it's more about getting out there, participating, putting your best foot forward, and showing your true colors, with people. It's not about who gets there first. It's about enjoying the ride with your crew.

On Personal Growth

"One of the oldest and most generous tricks that the universe plays on human beings is to bury strange jewels within us all, and then stand back to see if we can ever find them"

- ELIZABETH GILBERT, *Big Magic*

CACTUS FLOWER

Oil on Panel
30 x 30 in
October 2021

Colorjoy Series

ON PERSONAL GROWTH

In my old apartment I had a tiny cactus in my bathroom for over a year. I never watered it, cared for it in any way, and honestly thought it might be dead. Then, out of nowhere, one day I walked in and there was the most stunning, hot pink, gloriously bloomed flower bursting out of it, facing the sunshine from the window. It surprised the hell out of me. This happened right before I decided to pursue my art career full time, and it inspired me to believe that I, like this seemingly dead cactus, could bloom in the most unexpected of times, if I just keep my focus toward the light. And I have. This painting is a thank you to that cactus for the reminder.

LILY PAD

Acrylic and Gold Leaf on Canvas
36 x 24 in
October 2021

Colorjoy Series

ON PERSONAL GROWTH

Blue lotuses are rare. Beautiful symbols of healing, thriving after struggle, and purity of the mind, body, and soul. Blue lotuses have been used in ancient Egyptian times to heal anxiety and insomnia. I resonate with this little plant because every painting I finish feels like a new root in my own journey of healing and blossoming into the artist and person I long to be.

THE LEAP

Oil on Panel
24 x 24 in
December 2021

Defining Moments Series

ON PERSONAL GROWTH

When? When is the right time? When are
you taking that risk? Making a jump toward
the life you imagined? That you know is right
for you? Whether it's a job change, a move,
a travel experience, a proposal, or anything else..
Your gut has a way of telling you when these
moments are meant to happen. Life is short,
and you deserve one that's big, beautiful,
exciting, meaningful, and joyful.

SEEN & HEARD

Oil on Panel
12 x 12 in
December 2021

Defining Moments Series

ON PERSONAL GROWTH

I sincerely hope that everyone experiences the wonder that is being seen and heard for who they truly are in some way shape or form. Your loved ones, if they truly love you, should do this everyday. But it's something else when the outside world sees and hears you. The validation, the confidence boost, the pride, and, mostly, the relief that the youness of you won't be forgotten or left behind as the world keeps spinning.

INTUITION

Acrylic on Panel
24 x 24 in
December 2021

Defining Moments Series

ON PERSONAL GROWTH

In 2021 I trusted my gut more than anything. Every time I did that, things went well or got better, and I learned more about my potential. It was almost as if "follow your heart" and "trust your gut" became synonymous. My gut knew what my heart needed, and my head was often in the way. I learned that I can trust myself, even when navigating extremely intimidating uncharted waters.

24/7

Oil and Acrylic on Panel
96 x 3.5 in
January 2022

Unseen Lights Series

ON PERSONAL GROWTH

I am building my career, my life, and mental fortitude all with creative, exciting, calming, relaxing, invigorating, whatever-I-need-it-to-give-me, color. And I think about it 24/7. I used this board to test out color palettes over the course of my month long residency in Florida. Somehow, maybe subconsciously, I wound up with 24 palettes, made up of 7 colors each. The whole thing is a symbol for what's going on in my head at all hours of the day. The stuff you do without thinking sometimes shows you what youre really thinking.

NEW DAY

Oil and 3D Mixed Media on Panel
36 x 24 in
June 2022

Emergence Series

ON PERSONAL GROWTH

Everyday is a fresh start. There are plenty of things we can't control, but we can choose how to focus our perspective, our attention, our energy, and our gratitudes. Sunrise and sunset are perfect times of day to refocus, make those choices, and see the difference it makes in the next 24 hours. Our days turn into our weeks that turn into our lives. How you orient your mentality creates your future. This piece is different from every angle to reflect the many different perspectives and choices we are presented with every day.

SAPLING

Oil and 3D Mixed Media on Panel
36 x 24 in
June 2022

Emergence Series

ON PERSONAL GROWTH

In the forest of life, we all start as tiny seeds. In order to create strong stabilizing roots, and rise to our highest potential, we have to both endure the rains and soak up the rays, from all angles. Only then will we rise from seeds, to saplings, to trees, reaching, always, toward the sunshine.

CELESTIAL

Oil, 3D Mixed Media, and Silver Leaf on Panel
36 x 24 in
October 2022

Transcendence Series

ON PERSONAL GROWTH

How you rise matters. Sure, a rocket that shoots to the top in no time is impressive and all. But don't doubt the gratification, humilty, growth, and sustainability of a slow rise. A gradual ascension, like that of hot air balloon, let's you enjoy the view from every point along to the way to the top, making the perspective once you get there all the more rewarding.

EVOLUTION

Oil and Acrylic on Canvas
72 x 96 in
Febuary 2023

Evolve Series 202

ON PERSONAL GROWTH

True evolution is slow, gradual, and persistent, made up of repeated habits, small steps, commitment, and trust in the process. Much like each gradient in this piece. Sometimes I get frustrated at the slowness, but realizing I'm slowly building the best version of myself makes me very excited for the future at the same time.

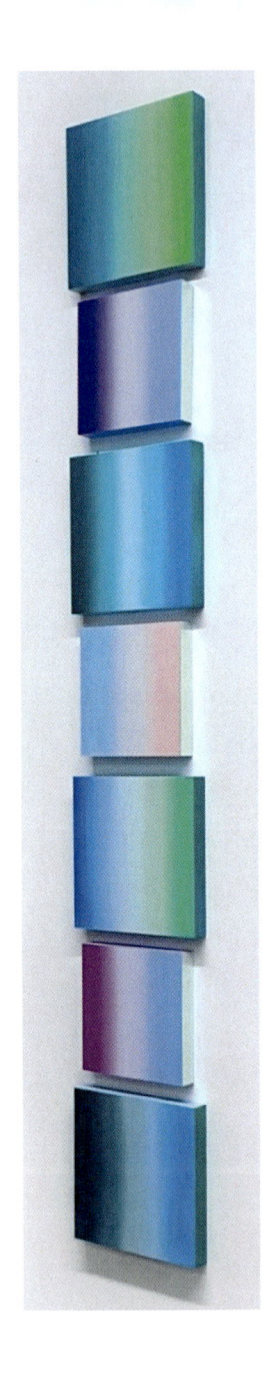

ALIGNEMENT

Oil and Vinyl on Panels
84 x 12 in
January 2023

Evolve Series

ON PERSONAL GROWTH

If you're anything like me, every new year you come up with a fresh new laundry list of goals, resolutions, things to change, and things to add to your life. And that's fine. But it adds a lot of pressure. And what's more, unless your habits, beliefs, and emotions are aligned in a way that makes those goals achievable, the pressure will mount into a burden. So, maybe instead of making resolutions right away, we should focus on alignment at the turn of the new year.

DIVERGENCE

Oil and Acrylic on Panel
48 x 36 in
January 2023

Evolve Series

ON PERSONAL GROWTH

Part of bravely becoming your best self is meeting yourself where you're at. If something that used to work for you doesn't sit right anymore, you have to diverge from it and explore something that honors your status quo. In other words, sometimes it is broke, and you have to fix it.

TREES TOMORROW

Oil and Tempered Glass on Panel
36 x 24 in
June 2022

Emergence Series

ON PERSONAL GROWTH

Since I began pursuing art professionally, a phrase I come back to often is "seeds today, trees tomorrow". Which pairs nicely with another favorite of mine: "to plant something is to believe in tomorrow". Focusing more on the seeds I plant each day than the rewards of that labor is a practice in delayed gratification, patience, belief in the future, and intrinsic motivation. I truly love the days where I feel like a humble farmer. Recently, trees have been not only sprouting, but blossoming all around me. And the sight is sweet as the day is long. But as glad as I am to see them, I still find more joy in the planting.

WABI-SABI

Acrylic and Tempered Glass on Panel
18 x 24 in
Febuary 2023

Evolve Series

ON PERSONAL GROWTH

I've spent far too much of my life chasing perfection. A lot of my work represents this, and I know that. Sometimes it's nice to feel like I can control something, but I'm exhausted. I told myself I would accept more beauty in imperfection in 2023, which aligns closely with the Japanese aesthetic of wabi-sabi. This piece is the most wabi-sabi thing I think I've ever made, but it didn't start that way. I originally designed it to cover up a dent in the surface. But as I went, more unfixable errors kept happening. Instead of giving up on it, I hand placed 1,272 glass crystals until it was done. Imperfect.. but done. I knew I wouldn't be able to tell myself I am growing out of my perfectionism unless I did.

GOLDEN RULE

Oil, 3D Mixed Media, and Mirror on Panel
24 x 18 in
April 2023

Reflections Series

ON PERSONAL GROWTH

You have everything you need to make big changes. Even total reversals. Nothing lasts forever, everything is temporary. Never settle for what is no longer serving you, it's just not worth it.

SKIPPER

Oil, 3D Mixed Media, and Mirror on Panel
12 x 12 in
August 2023

Sound Mind Series

ON PERSONAL GROWTH

You are the captain of your own life. Not your boss, not your partner, not your mother. You. Make sure you are able to make decisions that serve your own joy and purpose.

On Love

"The more I think it over, the more I feel that there is nothing more truly artistic than to love people."

- VINCENT VAN GOGH

COSMIC

Oil on Panel
30 x 30 in
December 2021

Defining Moments Series

Do you have someone in your life who you feel was brought into it by fate? By the stars aligning just right? Maybe you met when you least expected it, in a way you never could have imagined. Maybe you felt like you'd known them forever right away, and you feel like your best, most authentic self when you're together. If what you have feels unreal, effortless, and otherworldly all at the same time, then you do.

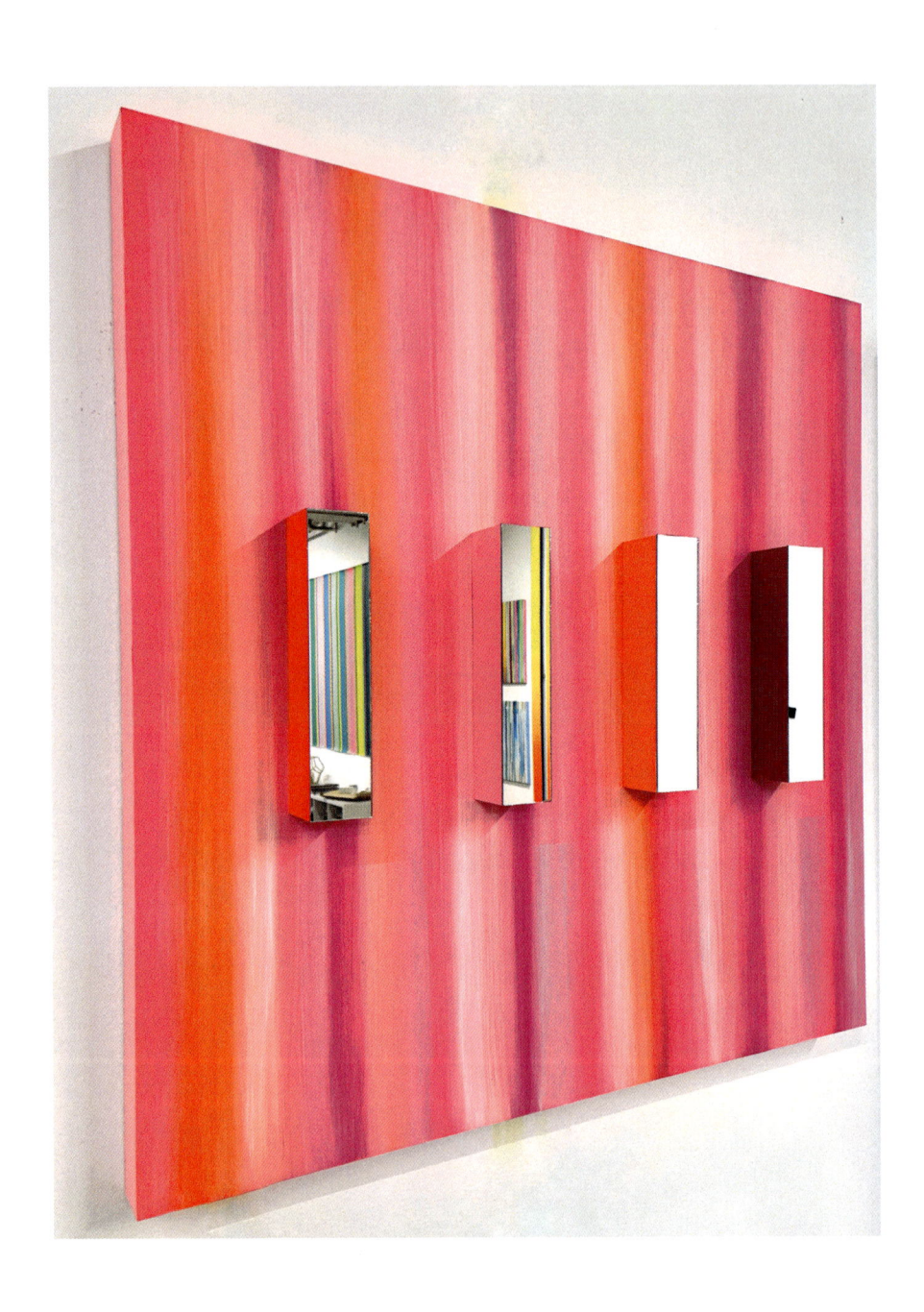

SELF L.O.V.E.

Oil, 3D Mixed Media, and Mirror on Panel
24 x 24 in
February 2023

Evolve Series

ON LOVE

The longest relationship you'll have in this life is with yourself. And yet self love can be a steep learning curve for a lot of us. I think it starts with a shift in focus. Usually we spend all day focusing on everything else, and #1 gets put on the back burner. In this piece, you get the reverse. Everything is blurry, except your beautiful self.

MIRROR MIRROR

Acrylic and 3D Mixed Media on Panel
24 x 48 in
February 2023

Evolve Series

ON LOVE

We often look in the mirror for answers. Who am I? What am I supposed to do with my life? When are things going to get better? Why is this so hard? We often look in and see ourselves as we are, right now. But I wish it were easier to look in and see all the individual moments that make up the sum total of who you are, and the progress you've made that will inform your future. Let's stop judging ourselves so hard for where we are. Let's celebrate the abundance of how much we've already done, and how much we will do, soon.

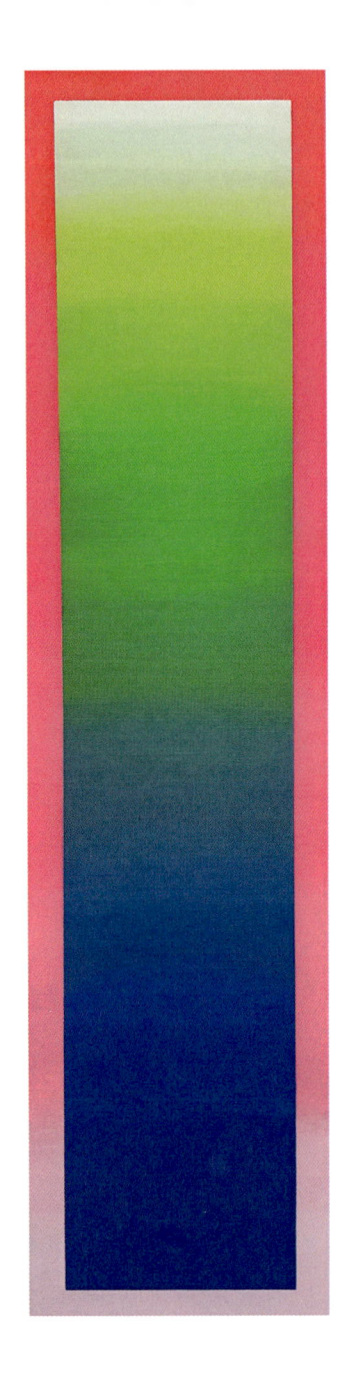

EMBRACE

Oil on Panel
48 x 12 in
February 2023

Evolve Series

ON LOVE

As we grow older we go through a lot of transitions, which are tough for me. Being selective about my surroundings and setting intentional boundaries helps a lot. But I'm willing to bet that whatever your transition is, the best thing to give yourself is the warm embrace of self love and grace throughout the process.

NUMBER ONE

Oil, 3D Mixed Media, and Mirror on Panel
40 x 30 in
May 2023

Reflections Series

ON LOVE

It's normal, healthy, and important to place yourself at the center. Self care is affirming each day that you are surrounded by love, and that love starts from within. Because we are all pink on the inside, and at the end of the day it's just us and the skin we're in against the world. That's why taking care of you, filling your cup before you serve others, that matters.

AURA

Oil, 3D Mixed Media, and Mirror on Panel
24 x 18 in
May 2023

Reflections Series

ON LOVE

What defines your aura more than your own self love, inner peace, and love for others?

SELF LOVE WALL

Oil, 3D Mixed Media, and Mirror on Panel
36 x 28 in
May 2023

Reflections Series　　　　　　　　　　　　　　　　　　　　230

ON LOVE

Big things are made up of many small things. Take life for example. Our lives are made up of days, made up of hours, made up of minutes, made up of moments. How we spend those moments matters. Are you spending them with self love? Authentically as you are? Not with selfie filters, those are lies. Take a look in the mirror. Just a little one is all you need. Know yourself and your true beauty. Be yourself. Act in a way that honors and loves that self. Fill your moments that way, and overtime you'll have a life full of love for yourself and others.

AWAY

Oil, 3D Mixed Media, and Mirror on Panel
36 x 36 in
August 2023

Sound Mind Series

ON LOVE

Never underestimate the power of getting away with a core group of loved ones. It doesn't really matter where, but something about being out on the water soothes the soul in a way that nothing else can. Plus, the ocean is as vast as the love that grows when you keep that small group of friends close by.

02539

Oil, 3D Mixed Media, and Mirror on Panel
18 x 24 in
August 2023

Sound Mind Series

ON LOVE

Edgartown is the reason I exist. My father's ancestors are from here. My mother's family has been vacationing here since the 70s. Their families met on this island when they were kids. Eventually, one summer, they fell in love and the rest is history. The island has always felt like home and I rely on it to restore my sound mind. It gives me brainspace to navigate tough choices in life. So using navigational flags to pay tribute just felt right.

OUT THERE

Oil on Panel
12 x 12 in
August 2023

Sound Mind Series

236

Venturing out on your own, whether it's for an hour, a day, or a year, can be scary. But exploring what this world has to offer teaches you who you are. And eventually, you learn how to love yourself, enjoy your own company, and learn what you can offer to someone else.

MOTHER'S LOVE

Acrylic on Canva
85 x55 in
May 2022

Mother's Day Series

238

ON LOVE

Just because she's not phsyically here anymore, doesn't mean I can't feel it everyday. It's in me. And sometimes it's as simple as being a bright spot in someone else's day to remember it.

Acknowledgements

Mom: Every time a moment of beauty or strength occurs in my life, I know it's because of you. Thank you for teaching me who I am from your lessons in life and your love from afar. **Dad:** My love for the written word undoubtedly comes from you. Thank you for modeling this skill for me my whole life - this book wouldn't exist without it. Thank you for always supporting my artistic endeavors with just as much zeal as everything else. As my college advisor once called me into his office to say, I really do "have an incredible father." **Alden:** My favorite person, the only one who has been there with me through it all (well, except those first 18 months). Thank you for being my #1 partner in crime through everything in this crazy life, this book journey included. **Isabelle:** Thank you for being the best, most fun, and supportive sister-in-law, I'm so grateful art brought us together - for life! To my Grandparents: **Grammie,** you are the reason I fell in love with making things in the first place. Thank you for warming up that freezing at-home pottery studio for us to play with clay as tots, and for being my favorite artist mentor all my life. **Grampie,** thank you for always reminding me that my successes are because of me, not luck. **Lovage,** thank you for being my #1 fan, showing me what it looks like to be an absolute Queen, and always reminding me how loved I am (lots of tickles). **Captain,** thank you for teaching me the spirit of adventure whether it be out to the nearest shoreline, worldly travel, or entrepreneurship. To my "bonus moms," **Alice, Leelee, Susan, Laurie, Annie, Tara, Ann, Anne:** Ellie knew I had plenty of female role models, but I don't think she knew that together you would supply the ultimate motherload (pun intended) of mentorship for being a fearless, feminine, powerhouse. Thank you all for being my lifelines. **Cousin Squad:** Thank you for being more like brothers and sisters. This life is a wild ride, but our togetherness always gives me comfort that no matter what everything will be ok. **Ann, Will, Kate, Juan:** I'm very grateful to call you family, and thank you for supporting me as such.

Danielle & Morgan: From being children in the gym to showing up at my very first Open Studio, you two are my best friends, my sisters, and have cheered me on every step of this journey. You lift me up from my low moments, and I don't know what I would do without you. **Cora:** I love the way we keep each other brave through our toughest moments, and there were plenty while working on this book. I am a stronger person because of our friendship and I'm grateful for you every day. **Ellen, Gina, Dani, Lauren:** Is there anything more precious than lifelong girlfriends? I think not. Thank you for being there as I grew from gymnast to swimmer to teacher to artist and loving me as Katie the whole time.

To the **Darien YMCA:** Growing up in the gym gave me so much more than muscles: thank you for giving me the building blocks to meet every challenge in life with grace, strength, and balance. **Linda Yoffee:** Thank you for authentically listening and enthusiastically celebrating all your elementary art students, including me - you helped build humans who knew art was valuable. **Darien High School:** Thank you for providing rigorous challenges in all departments and programs - I may have started as an athlete but my journey as an artist grew from building blocks in high school. Go Blue! **Jaclyn Sammis:** You are far more than my AP Art teacher: back in school you pushed me hard but always kept it fun, when I started my teaching career you took me on right away as a mentee, and today I'm proud to call you a deeply cherished friend. Thank you for being everything. **Colby:** I wouldn't be who I am today without this incredible school and the way it builds a community of people who are just as kind as they are brilliant. Thank you for giving me wings to pursue my passions and inspiring me to do meaningful, impactful work. Go Mules! **Bevin:** You taught me how to speak my language. Thank you for always reminding me of the origins of my authenticity - I need only think of you to remember what matters most. **Aquamules:** Not only were you a second family who got me through the hardest year of my life, you also taught me true grit. Thank you for teaching me to just keep swimming. **Vince:** We went from being kids at Colby to adults in Boston, teaching each other how to grow up and chase our dreams at the same time. Thank you for keeping me Katie during the roughest years of my life and for launching my online presence as an artist before I could even dream of it. **Tufts:** Thank you for letting me apply late! I learned a love for teaching art from the wonderful people at the Tufts SMFA, (**Susan, Kay, Pam**) and it is an ever-evolving identity that endures in many forms today. **Simone, Anastasia, Joanie:** I don't think I would have survived our Master's program without you!

Otis Elementary School: Staff: you taught me how to bring my best self to students, in and out of school. To my former students: you inspire me to be the best artist I can be, I hope you know I am always here for you. **Rose Leitner:** Thank you for everything you taught me about Boston artist life and for introducing me to SoWa, it gave me my starting point! **Sharon and Kim:** If you two hadn't taken a chance on me, I don't know if any of this would have happened. Thank you both for sharing my first studio with me, being early mentors, and for your continued friendship. To my Boston art friends: **Joe,** Thank you for believing in my full-time career before I did, and helping me plant the seeds that turned into today's trees. I am forever grateful for you. **Matt & Mike,** It's not easy to make friends as an adult, but you two are as true as they come. Thank you for literally helping me see myself as an artist with all your photography skills. This cover (front and back) wouldn't exist without you! **Sadie,** I'm so thankful Colby brought us together, thank you for being a brilliant intern and an even better friend.

Brittany, Marie, Cheryl, Mary, Sara, Duken, Paul, Debbie, Lauren, Mae, Evan, Katherine, Cynthia, Mia, Sorin, Jenny, Liza, My SoWa years were my launching pad, and your friendship was the warmest, most wonderful part of it all, thank you. **Stina, Lily, Luke, Grace, Colleen, Eric, Katie, Mike, Henry:** It's not lost on me how special it is to have reconnected in adult art life after we all graduated from DHS at different times. It brings me joy to watch you all thrive in your own ways. **Alice:** You didn't think I would forget that you were my very first commission client did you? Thank you for giving me my first chance, followed shortly by the woman who started the snowball: **Susie Lindenberg.** Thank you!

Thank you to all the curators, dealers, gallerists, and industry leaders I've had the pleasure of working with, learning from, or collaborating with: **Danielle Krysa, Marina Press Granger, Minnie Park, Christine O'Donnell, Peter Hopkins, Chris Morse, Robin Nagle, Jhenn Watts, David Wallis.** Women Entrepreneurs: All of you (whether I've met you online or in person) inspire me, but the ones who have grown into true friends, **Paige Lindsey, Dori Broudy, Ellie Hanes, Claudia Tolay, Clare Murray, Mairead McClarence, Pamela Vossler, Fiona Leonard,** I'm so grateful for you. **Marc Fattahi, Katie Kidder, Andre Arguimbeau:** Thank you for individually hosting all three of my solo shows to date: *Colorjoy*, *Vineyard Musings*, and *Sound Mind*, respectively. I am so grateful to all of you and your incredible generosity, patronage, and support. Thank you to **Leelee Klein, Alice Clark, Linda Smith, Stina Arstorp, Meg Mercier, and Kristie Godina** for assisting greatly in these huge endeavors. **Sandy & Shiran:** I was able to move my career and life back home to Connecticut because of you and the amazing place you have created at the Knowlton. Thank you for making me and my art feel at home from day one.

To my guinea pig readers: **Ken, Ann, Alden, Isabelle, Laurie, Jacyln, Danielle, Cora, Kim:** Thank you for helping me take these words from personal catharsis to an accessible story. **Olivia:** It was so special to work on this book with you. We've been teammates in the gym and the pool, and I knew you were the perfect designer for the job. Thank you for your brilliance in bringing my vision to life!

Finally, to my beloved collectors, past, present, and future:

Please know that you are the reason I can put my whole heart into growing this work, spreading this message of hope, and advocating for a healthier future. When you invest in me, you are investing in a mission for positive change. You are keeping a female-owned business alive. You are showing the next generation that art and artists are valuable and essential to our enriched cultures, histories, and livelihoods. You are allowing vulnerable stories to be told, shared, and passed on. You are fostering a culture of openness, mental wellness, and joy. You are nurturing joy itself. You are creating hope for a future where creativity and mental health are valued just as much as financial prosperity and productivity.

On a more personal note, you are helping me share my mom's legacy as loudly as possible. I think she can hear us, and I cannot tell you how much it means to me.

Thank you is not a strong enough phrase to express my gratitude. Let this book be a start, and the rest of my career be the continuance.

Sources (Recommended Reads!)

Doyle, Glennon. *Untamed*. Dial Press, 2020.

Gilbert, Elizabeth. *Big Magic: Creative Living Beyond Fear*. Riverhead Books, 2015.

Lee, Ingrid Fetell. *Joyful: The Surprising Power of Ordinary Things to Create Extraordinary Happiness*. Little, Brown and Company, 2018.

Nagoski, Emily. *Burnout: The Secret to Unlocking to Stress Cycle*. Ballantine Books, (Reprint Edition), 2020.

Nichols, Wallace J. *Blue Mind: The Surprising Science That Shows How Being Near, In, On, or Under Water Can Make You Happier, Healthier, More Connected, and Better at What You Do*. Little, Brown Spark, 2014.

Rubin, Gretchen. *The Happiness Project: Or, Why I Spent a Year Trying to Sing in the Morning, Clean My Closets, Fight Right, Read Aristotle, and Generally Have More Fun*. Harper, 2009.

About the Artist

Katie Southworth is an award-winning, full-time, independent artist working in Bridgeport, Connecticut. Her work harnesses the power of color to promote joy, mindfulness, and mental well-being.

Hundreds of her original paintings have been sold to private and public collections across 50+ cities nationwide and abroad. Her work has been exhibited at international art fairs including Aqua Art Miami, and has been featured in international and fine art publications including British Vogue and "Create!" Magazine. She donates a percentage of her sales to the American Foundation for Suicide Prevention annually.

Dr. Roy G. Biv; Healing from Trauma One Colorful Painting at a Time, An Artist's Journey to Hope and Joy is her first book.

Although her career started in Boston, Katie is thrilled to have moved back to her home state of Connecticut, near to her closest family and friends. When she is not working Katie enjoys quality time with loved ones, multiple forms of exercise and sports, reading books, cooking new recipes, buying fresh flowers, petting as many dogs as possible, spending time by the water, and recharging on Martha's Vineyard.

Katie's studio is open to visitors and collectors by appointment and several times a year during Open Studio events. She sells original work and takes commissions on a case-by-case basis, including indoor and outdoor murals. Katie has experience as a visiting artist in schools and health institutions and welcomes teachers and administrators to reach out about collaborations, workshops, and talks.

Follow Katie's journey at **@katiesouthworth_art** and subscribe to her mailing list at **www.katiesouthworthart.com/contact** to stay informed on new releases, upcoming shows & events, and exciting announcements.

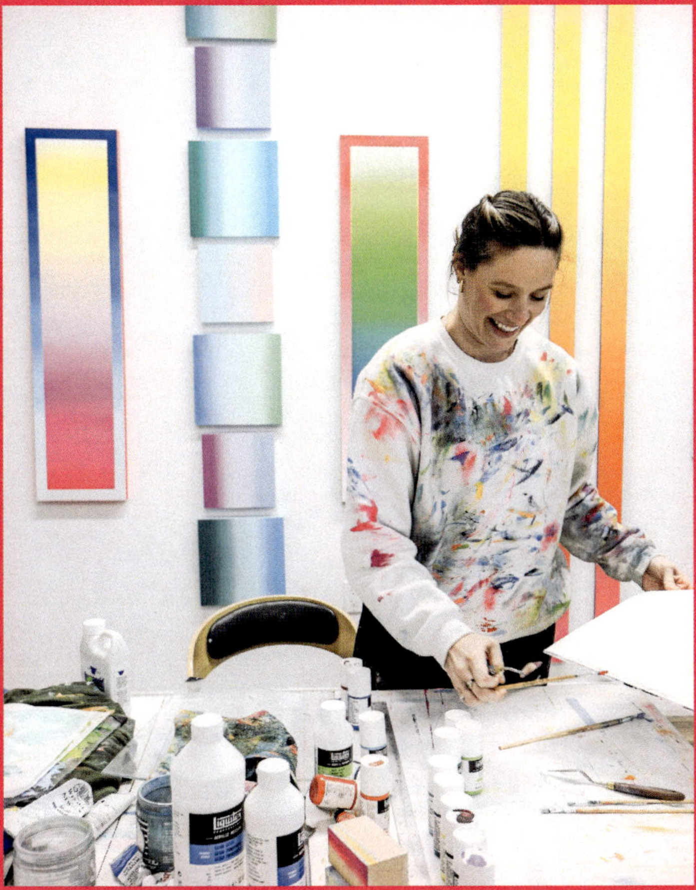

Made in the USA
Monee, IL
05 September 2024

615b630f-cd9d-49dd-9065-fa9dca2f6324R01